KV-370-936

WE'D LIKE TO HEAR FROM YOU!

As part of our continuing effort to produce books of the highest possible quality, Que would like to hear your comments. To stay competitive, we *really* want you, as a computer book reader and user, to let us know what you like or dislike most about this book or other Que products.

You can mail comments, ideas, or suggestions for improving future editions to the address below, or send us a fax at 317-581-4663. For the online inclined, Macmillan Computer Publishing has a forum on CompuServe (type **GO QUEBOOKS** at any prompt) through which our staff and authors are available for questions and comments. The address of our Internet site is **http://www.mcp.com/que** (World Wide Web).

In addition to exploring our forum, please feel free to contact me personally to discuss your opinions of this book: I'm at **75703,3251** on CompuServe, and I'm **lgentry@que.mcp.com** on the Internet.

Although we cannot provide general technical support, we're happy to help you resolve problems you encounter related to our books, disks, or other products. If you need such assistance, please contact our Tech Support department at 800-545-5914 ext. 3833.

To order other Que or Macmillan Computer Publishing books or products, please call our Customer Service department at 800-835-3202 ext. 666.

Thanks in advance—your comments will help us to continue publishing the best books available on computer topics in today's market.

Lorna Gentry
Product Development Specialist
Que Corporation
201 West 103rd Street
Indianapolis, Indiana 46290
USA

16:10

10

MINUTE GUIDE TO

CC:MAIL 7

by Elaine Marmel

QUE®

A Division of Macmillan Computer Publishing
201 West 103rd Street, Indianapolis, IN 46290 USA

©1996 by Que® Corporation

International Standard Book Number: 0-7897-0994-5
Library of Congress Catalog Card Number: 96-70773

98 97 96   8 7 6 5 4 3 2 1

Interpretation of the printing code: the rightmost double-digit number is the year of the book's first printing; the rightmost single-digit number is the number of the book's printing. For example, a printing code of 96-1 shows that this copy of the book was printed during the first printing of the book in 1996.

Printed in the United States of America

Publisher Roland Elgey

Vice President and Publisher Lynn E. Zingraf

Editorial Services Director Elizabeth Keaffaber

Managing Editor Michael Cunningham

Acquisitions Editor Martha O'Sullivan

Technical Specialist Nadeem Muhammed

Product Development Specialist Lorna Gentry

Technical Editor Laurie Ann Ulrich

Production Editor Tom Lamoureux

Book Designer Barbara Kordesh

Cover Designer Dan Armstrong

Production Angela Calvert, Tricia Flodder, Janelle Herber, Linda Knose, Christy Wagner

Indexer Robert Long

CONTENTS

INTRODUCTION

cc:Mail is an easy-to-use electronic mail system that also enables you to participate in bulletin boards, import and export files, send attachments, and more.

THE WHAT AND WHY OF cc:MAIL

Whether you're a member of a small office or a large, multi-building corporation, you can use e-mail (electronic mail) to communicate with your co-workers and colleagues. E-mail saves time and energy during your busy work day. Just imagine the time you'll save by sending a memo, asking a co-worker some questions, dispatching sales reports, and picking up the accounting sheets, without leaving your desk. Use cc:Mail to communicate and share data and files through the network.

You might think that since cc:Mail can accomplish so much that it would be hard to use. Not so. cc:Mail runs in Windows 95 (or Windows NT or on Windows 3.11) as a graphical user interface (GUI). GUI means Windows provides a workspace that is easy to use and easy to understand and cc:Mail takes advantage of that workspace. Additionally, cc:Mail is similar to other Lotus products for Windows in that it uses SmartIcons as tool buttons, and other on-screen tools that you may already be familiar with.

 Graphical User Interface   A GUI (pronounced "gooey") makes interacting with your computer easy. You usually use a mouse to point at and select icons (small pictures that most often represent files or application programs), and you choose operations (commands from menus) to perform on those icons. A GUI is an alternative to a command-line interface, such as DOS, where text commands are entered from the keyboard.

Why use cc:Mail? cc:Mail makes your every day work faster and easier. With cc:Mail, you can:

- Write and send messages to your co-workers without leaving your desk

- Read, print, and answer messages from others in your organization

- Attach files, import files, and export files to co-workers

- Join on-line bulletin boards to share your ideas with others

With just a little effort, you can learn cc:Mail. It's fast, easy, fun, and you'll be pleased with the advantages and benefits you'll receive from the program.

This book concentrates on using cc:Mail on a Windows 95 workstation although the procedures for most tasks are the same for other Windows products.

WHY THE 10 MINUTE GUIDE TO CC:MAIL?

The *10 Minute Guide to cc:Mail 7* can save even more of your precious time. Each lesson is designed to be completed in 10 minutes or less, so you'll be up to snuff in basic cc:Mail skills quickly.

Though you can jump between lessons, starting at the beginning is a good plan. The bare-bones basics are covered first; more advanced topics are covered later.

CONVENTIONS USED IN THIS BOOK

To help you move through the lessons easily, these conventions are used:

- On-screen text   On-screen text appears in **bold** type.

- What you type   Information you type appears in **bold, color** type.

- Items you select   Commands, options, and icons you select or keys you press appear in color type.

In telling you to choose menu commands, this book uses the format menu title, menu command. For example, the statement "choose File, Properties" means to "open the File menu and select the Properties command."

In addition to these conventions, the *10 Minute Guide to cc:Mail 7* uses the following icons to identify helpful information:

Plain English   New or unfamiliar terms are defined in (you got it) "plain English."

Timesaver Tips   Look here for ideas that cut corners and confusion.

Panic Button   This icon identifies areas where new users often run into trouble, and offers practical solutions to those problems.

TRADEMARKS

All terms mentioned in this book that are known to be trademarks have been appropriately capitalized. Que cannot attest to the accuracy of this information. Use of a term in this book should not be regarded as affecting the validity of any trademark or service mark.

NAVIGATING CC:MAIL

In this lesson, you'll learn to start and exit cc:Mail, log in to mail, understand the mailbox window, and use the mouse and keyboard to navigate cc:Mail.

STARTING CC:MAIL

Before you start cc:Mail, the computer containing your network's post office must be up and running. The post office is usually located on the network file server or mail server. If the computer containing the post office is not running, you won't see any new mail or be able to send any mail messages in cc:Mail.

Mail   E-mail, or electronic mail, refers to messages you send back and forth to others attached to a network of computers.

Post office   The cc:Mail post office is a folder located on the network or mail server in which your mail is stored until you retrieve the incoming messages, or until the people to whom you have sent mail retrieve their messages.

System administrator   The person responsible for running, maintaining, and troubleshooting your company's network.

File server/Mail server   A computer responsible for collecting and distributing files and/or mail to all members of the network.

Network   Multiple computers attached via cables (or phone lines) that can share resources such as files, folders, printers, and so on.

Post Office Not Running? You can create and send messages while the computer containing the post office is not running. cc:Mail will store the messages you send in the Outbox and send them later, when the post office is available.

TIP   **Questions?** You can ask your system administrator when you have questions about the cc:Mail post office.

To start the cc:Mail program, follow these steps:

1. Choose the Start button on the Windows 95 taskbar.

2. Choose Programs, and then the folder that contains your cc:Mail program. If cc:Mail was installed using default suggestions, you'll find an icon for cc:Mail in the Lotus Applications folder.

3. Choose the Lotus cc_Mail 7.0 icon. You'll see the Lotus cc:Mail dialog box, which you use to log in to cc:Mail. We'll discuss logging in next.

TIP   **Alternate Start** You can, alternatively, use the Switch to Lotus cc:Mail SmartIcon on the Lotus SmartCenter bar, at the top of your screen. The SmartCenter might or might not be available to you, depending on your setup.

LOGGING IN

Each time you start cc:Mail, you must log in using the dialog box that appears immediately after you complete the previous steps. Logging in connects you to the computer containing the cc:Mail post office so you can send and receive mail. When you log in, you use a profile that describes you, and you can create separate profiles to log in over your company's network or using a modem from a laptop or home computer. The profile contains, at a minimum, the following information:

- **Login Name**   Generally, you log in using your name. Your name must appear in the appropriate order (first name first, last name first, or as specified by your system administrator).

- **Password**   A combination of letters and numbers assigned exclusively to you; you must follow case and character exactly. As you type, cc:Mail fills in asterisks so that no one can read your password as you enter it.

- **P.O. Path**   The location of the folder containing the cc:Mail post office. The P.O. path usually includes two back slashes (signifying a network server), the server name followed by a back slash, and the post office folder name.

If you are unsure of any of these, see your system administrator.

 Modems   If you choose to create a profile that uses a modem, you'll need additional information about your modem. See your system administrator for help.

The first time you log in, cc:Mail displays a wizard that helps you set up profile information. Once you complete the wizard, cc:Mail stores your profile so that you don't need to supply the information again. Instead, you just need to select your profile from a list of profiles available in the opening dialog box. If you start cc:Mail and don't see your profile, follow these steps to complete the wizard and set up a network connection:

1. In the Login/Profile name text box, type your name as you want it to appear in this list box. This name *does not* need to match the format of your user name as specified by your system administrator.

2. In the Password text box, type the password your system administrator gave you.

3. Choose OK. You'll see a dialog box that explains that you entered the name of a user who has not logged on from this computer previously and you're about to create a new profile for this user.

4. Choose Yes. cc:Mail displays the first box of the profile setup wizard.

5. In the first dialog box of profile setup wizard, you decide whether you will connect to the cc:Mail post office using a network or mobile connection. Since we're setting up a network connection profile, choose Network.

6. Choose Next. You'll see the second dialog box in the profile wizard, in which you must specify the location of the post office folder (see Figure 1.1).

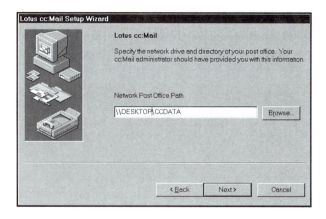

Figure 1.1   In this dialog box, supply the location of the cc:Mail post office folder.

7. After you specify the folder containing the cc:Mail post office, choose Next. You'll see a dialog box in which you supply your log-in name and password. You *must* supply your name here using the format your system administrator specified.

8. Choose Next. cc:Mail displays the last box of the profile setup wizard, which shows you the information you've already entered, and lets you make changes as needed.

9. After you verify that the information is correct, choose Next. The cc:Mail window appears on-screen.

Once you've set up a profile, follow these steps to start cc:Mail and log in:

1. Use the Start button to display the Start menu.

2. Highlight Programs in the Start list.

3. Find the folder containing cc:Mail and highlight it.

4. Click cc:Mail. The log-in dialog box appears.

5. Choose your profile from the list available in the Log-in Name list box.

6. Enter your password in the Password text box.

7. Choose OK. The cc:Mail window appears on-screen.

 TIP **Log-in Shortcut** If you don't fill in your password and press Enter, cc:Mail will display another dialog box. In this box you can type your password and check a check box that tells cc:Mail to "remember" the password. In the future you will only need to press **Enter** in the log-in dialog box to start the program.

UNDERSTANDING THE MAILBOX WINDOW

In the Mailbox window, you'll see any messages you might have received, plus SmartIcons and other tools you can use to manipulate and manage your mail. The Mailbox window is divided into two panes: the folder pane and the message list pane (see Figure 1.2).

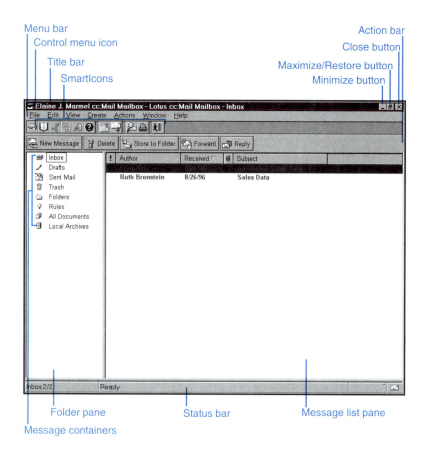

Menu bar
Control menu icon
Title bar
SmartIcons

Action bar
Close button
Maximize/Restore button
Minimize button

Message containers
Folder pane
Status bar
Message list pane

FIGURE 1.2 The Mailbox window displays your messages and the places to store them.

Table 1.1 describes the components of the cc:Mail Mailbox window.

TABLE 1.1 MAILBOX WINDOW COMPONENTS

COMPONENT	DESCRIPTION
Title bar	Displays the name of the program, the name of the active window (Mailbox #1), and the Control Menu, Minimize, Maximize/Restore, and Close buttons.

COMPONENT	DESCRIPTION
Menu bar	Displays menus that present related commands for working in cc:Mail.
SmartIcon bar	Contains shortcut tool buttons you can click to carry out common commands.
Action bar	Contains more shortcut buttons you can click to carry out tasks common to the current window.
Folder Pane	Provides access to various cc:Mail message containers, including the Inbox, Drafts, Sent Mail, Trash, any private folders, rules, all documents, and archive files.
Message List Pane	Displays information found within any one container located in the Folder pane.
Scrollbar	Enables you to scroll, or move, though a window when you cannot see all of the contents; click the up or down arrow at either end of the scroll bar or slide the scroll box.
Status bar	Displays information about your current session, such as number of messages, folders, bulletin board messages, time, and date.

The Folder pane includes icons called *message containers*. You can think of message containers as folders that you can use to store and organize your messages. The following list describes each container in the folder pane:

- **Inbox**   Stores the incoming mail.

- **Drafts**   Use this container to store unfinished messages you want to open and complete later.

- **Sent Mail**   This log automatically stores copies of any messages you send (unless you tell it to do otherwise).

- **Trash** Use this container to store any file you want to delete. You can store the files here for a while to make sure you no longer need them before you delete messages permanently; or you can delete files from the trash immediately.

- **Folders** Add your own personal folders (up to 199) for managing and storing the messages you've received.

- **Rules** An area you can use to store instructions that automate tasks.

- **All Documents** This container shows all the messages and rules in your mailbox.

- **Local Archives** An area for long-term storage of messages on your hard disk. You can add messages to an archive but you cannot delete messages once they've been archived.

 Network Space When you create folders to store and manage your messages, cc:Mail places those folders on the network drive, not your local drive. Make sure there is enough space on the network drive before you save a lot of messages. You may want to archive messages instead.

USING THE MOUSE TO GET AROUND IN cc:MAIL

You use the mouse to perform most actions in Windows applications, and cc:Mail 7 is no exception. With the mouse, you can select a SmartIcon, button, or a window, move messages around, open and close containers and messages, and more.

You'll use pointing and clicking to accomplish these tasks. For example, you open items by double-clicking them, and you move items by dragging the mouse and the item.

To *point* to an object (icon, window border, menu, and so on), move the mouse across your desk or mouse pad until the on-screen mouse pointer touches the object.

Cornered Your Mouse?   You can pick up the mouse and reposition it if you run out of room on your desk.

To *click*, point the mouse pointer at the object and then press and release the left mouse button. If the object is an icon or window, for example, it becomes *selected,* or *highlighted*, when you click on it. If you select an icon, an action will take place.

When you *double-click* an item, you point to the item and press and release the left mouse button twice quickly. Double-clicking is often a shortcut to performing a task; for example, you can open a message or window by double-clicking its icon.

You can use the mouse to move an object (usually a window, dialog box, or message) to a new position on-screen. You do this by clicking and dragging the object. To drag an object to a new location on-screen, point to the object, press and hold the left mouse button, move the mouse to a new location, and then release the mouse button. The object moves with the mouse arrow as you drag it.

You also can perform certain actions, such as selecting multiple items or copying items, by performing one or two additional mouse operations. Shift+Click means to press and hold the Shift key and then click the left mouse button; Ctrl+Click means to press and hold the Ctrl key and then click the left mouse button. Although the result of either of these actions depends on where you are in the application, usually Shift+Click selects multiple items that are contiguous in a list and Ctrl+Click selects multiple items that are not contiguous.

Using the Keyboard with cc:Mail

You can use the keyboard to work in cc:Mail; however, it is much easier to use the mouse for most procedures. This section introduces the commonly used keys; however, this book concentrates on the use of the mouse in all lessons unless a keyboard shortcut would be easier.

When you want to open a menu, press the Alt key to activate the menu bar, then press the key representing the underlined letter in the menu name; for example, press Alt+F to open the File menu. To activate a command, press Alt and the underlined letter in the command, such as the C in Close.

cc:Mail provides many keyboard shortcuts, such as Ctrl+M to create a new message, and Del to delete a message. You'll find these shortcuts listed on menus to the right of the command you want to perform. Remember the shortcut for the next time you want to perform a command.

Generally, you can quickly move from one pane to another, one option to another in a dialog box, and so on using the F6 key. Within a list, use the direction arrow keys to move around.

Press Enter to accept changes in a dialog box or press the Escape key to cancel changes. **Enter** also opens applications, windows, and messages that are selected. The **Escape** key also cancels menus and closes windows.

EXITING CC:MAIL

Before exiting cc:Mail, make sure you save any unsaved new messages to the draft folder or that you send your messages across the network. For more information, see Lessons 5 and 7.

To exit cc:Mail, choose File, Exit. A confirmation dialog box appears; choose Yes to exit or No to cancel the command.

In this lesson, you learned to start, navigate, and exit cc:Mail. In the next lesson, you'll learn to use menus, commands, dialog boxes, SmartIcons, and the status bar.

GETTING STARTED WITH cc:MAIL

In this lesson, you'll learn to use menus and commands, open and navigate dialog boxes, use SmartIcon shortcuts, and find information with the status bar.

OPENING MENUS AND SELECTING MENU COMMANDS

cc:Mail supplies *pull-down menus* just like most Windows applications. Each menu contains a list of commands that relate to the operation of cc:Mail; for example, the Edit menu contains such commands as Cut, Copy, Paste, Clear, and so on.

Pull-Down Menu Words on the menu bar that contain lists of commands or actions, related to the menu; a menu pulls- or drops-down when you activate it with the mouse or the keyboard.

OPENING MENUS

To open a menu, click the mouse pointer on the menu name in the menu bar. The menu drops down to display a list of related commands (see Figure 2.1).

Keyboard Shortcut You also can open a menu by pressing the Alt key and then by pressing the underlined letter in the menu name (which is known as the *hot key*, or *accelerator key*, for the command); for example, to open the File menu, press Alt+F.

Dimmed commands

Ellipsis   Arrows

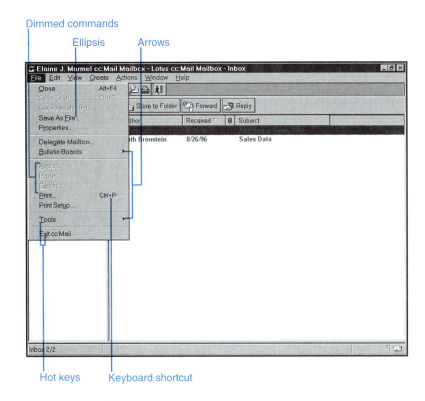

Hot keys   Keyboard shortcut

FIGURE 2.1   Menus contain commands that make your work easier in cc:Mail.

SELECTING COMMANDS

To select a command using the mouse, click the command with the mouse pointer. To select a command using the keyboard, open the menu containing the command using either the mouse or the keyboard technique you learned in the previous section. Then, press the hot key of the command you want. The appearance of the command on the menu gives you an indication as to what will happen when you activate the command. Table 2.1 describes the way a command might appear in a menu.

Using Keyboard Shortcuts to Select Commands   You can use key combinations to choose some commands. These keyboard shortcuts appear to the right of the command on the menu, but you must press the shortcut key combination while menus are closed (refer to Figure 2.1). Don't worry—you'll eventually memorize the keyboard shortcuts you use most. To use a keyboard shortcut, press and hold the first key listed and then press the second key. For example, to select the Copy command on the Edit menu using the keyboard shortcut Ctrl+C, press and hold the Ctrl key and then press C.

TABLE 2.1   COMMAND APPEARANCE ON A MENU

ELEMENT	DESCRIPTION
Arrow	Indicates that another menu, called a *secondary* or *cascading menu*, will appear if you select that command.
Ellipsis	Indicates that a dialog box will appear if you select that command.
Hot key	The keyboard character you press to activate the menu; choose this command to use the keyboard instead of the mouse.
Check mark	Indicates a command that is selected or active.
Shortcut	Indicates a keyboard shortcut you can use to choose the command; you cannot use the shortcut if the menu is open.
Dimmed command	Indicates that the command cannot be accessed at the current time; for example, you cannot paste information if you haven't previously copied information.

Cancel a Menu   To cancel a menu, point the mouse on a blank area of the workspace and click once. Or, press the Esc key twice.

USING DIALOG BOXES

When you select many menu commands, a dialog box appears that you can use to set more options and choices related to the menu command. Each dialog box has elements you need to understand before you can use them.

Figure 2.2 shows the Print Header Options dialog box with some common elements you will see in cc:Mail dialog boxes, as described in Table 2.2.

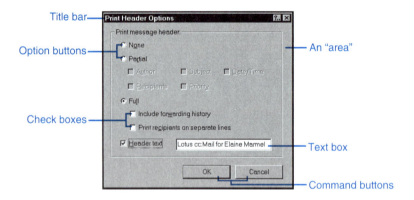

FIGURE 2.2   Use dialog boxes to make additional choices related to the selected menu command.

TABLE 2.2   DIALOG BOX ELEMENTS

ELEMENT	DESCRIPTION
Title bar	Indicates the name of the dialog box; often used in instructions: "In the Print Header Options dialog box, choose...."

ELEMENT	DESCRIPTION
Drop-down list box	Displays a list of options one at a time unless you click the down arrow to the right of the box; if you do, a list drops down.
List box	Displays a list of options; in this box, you can see more than one choice at a time.
Scroll bars	Enable you to display additional items in a list box; click the up or down arrow to see more.
Text box	Enables you to enter a selection by typing it in the box.
Command button	A rectangular button with a label such as OK or Cancel; command buttons execute your dialog box selections, cancel your selections, or bring up another, related dialog box (see the list following this table).
Check box	A small box beside an option; clicking the check box places a check mark in the box and selects the option; if the box already contains a check, clicking the box removes the check from the box and clears the selection of the option.
Option buttons	A set of round buttons; in any one area, you can select only one option button. A selected option button contains a black dot in the center of the white circle.
Area	A boxed section that contains related options or check boxes, usually titled.

To use a dialog box, you make your selections as described in Table 2.2 and then choose a command button by clicking it. The following are some common command buttons:

- Buttons labeled **OK**, **Done**, or **Close** will accept the selections you've made and close the dialog box.

- The **Cancel** button cancels changes you've made in the dialog box and closes it.

- **Options** or other buttons with an **ellipsis** following the button's name display another dialog box.

- **Save** or other buttons with only a command on them perform that command.

- **Help** displays information about the dialog box and its options.

 Can't Close the Dialog Box   When you've opened a dialog box, you must cancel or accept the changes you've made and close the box before continuing work in cc:Mail. To close the dialog box, press Esc or use the command buttons or the Close button.

USING ACTION BAR AND SMARTICON SHORTCUTS

cc:Mail includes an Action bar that contains icons you can use to perform common tasks quickly. While using cc:Mail, the icons you see on the Action bar change, depending on your task and your location in the cc:Mail program. For example, in most of the boxes in the folder pane of the Mailbox window, you'll see icons on the Action bar to create a new message, reply to or forward a message, delete a message or move the message to another folder. If, however, you choose **Trash** in the Folder pane, the Action bar changes to include only one icon: Empty Trash. Similarly, if you change to a different window in cc:Mail, the icons on the Action bar will change.

You'll also see SmartIcons in cc:Mail—shortcut buttons you'll also find in other Lotus applications. To find out what a SmartIcon represents, slide the mouse pointer over the icon (without clicking) and a description appears (called a "tool tip") that explains the icon's function. Figure 2.3 shows a ToolTip for the Open Address Book command. To use a SmartIcon, point the mouse pointer at the icon and click.

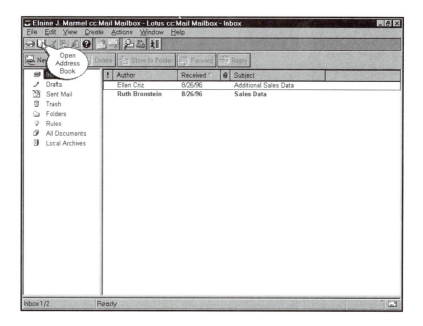

FIGURE 2.3   Use SmartIcon tool tips to find out what icons do.

GETTING INFORMATION FROM THE STATUS BAR

In the lower-left corner of the status bar, you'll see the status of the Inbox. Next to the folder name (Inbox), you'll see a fraction. OK, it's not *really* a fraction, it's two numbers that reflect your message count. The first number represents the number of messages that you have not yet read. The second number represents the total number of messages you have in the folder.

In this lesson, you learned to use menus and commands, dialog boxes, SmartIcons, and the status bar. In the next lesson, you'll learn to use cc:Mail's Help feature.

LESSON 3

GETTING HELP

In this lesson, you'll learn to use cc:Mail's Help features, including Guide Me, the search feature, Index, and Find.

USING THE GUIDE ME FEATURE

Guide Me is cc:Mail's context-sensitive Help feature. Use Guide Me when you're not sure of the next step. Say you opened an e-mail message but are unsure of how to reply to the message. You can open Guide Me for a list of suggestions: close the message, delete the message, reply to the message, forward the message, and so on. From within the Help Guide Me window, you select the help you want and cc:Mail displays the step-by-step procedures.

 Context-Sensitive Help Help for the specific subject on which you're working, whether you're in a dialog box, mailbox, address book, or other area of cc:Mail.

You can use Guide Me at any time or place within cc:Mail. To use Guide Me, follow these steps:

1. In the area you have a question about, press F1. Figure 3.1 shows the cc:Mail Help screen you see if you press F1 with a message in the mailbox selected.

2. In the cc:Mail Help box, click anywhere on the type of help you want. Figure 3.2 shows the result of choosing Reply to a Message.

Click a button to jump to step-by-step help.

FIGURE 3.1   Guide Me helps you decide the next step.

TIP

Always on Top   The Help window stays on top so that you can read the procedures as you follow them in the program. You can minimize the window if you find it gets in your way; click the Minimize button in the upper-right corner (the one with the underscore in it).

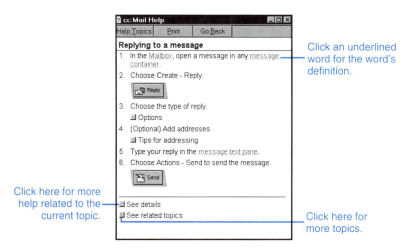

Click an underlined word for the word's definition.

Click here for more help related to the current topic.

Click here for more topics.

FIGURE 3.2   Read step-by-step instructions on any procedure.

3. Click the Close (X) button to close the Help window when you're done.

 TIP   **Guide Me**   You can also display Guide Me help by selecting the Help menu and clicking the Guide Me command.

Getting Help

cc:Mail provides an in-depth help system that you can use in three different ways. You can search for help using **Help's Contents** tab, which is like the table of contents of a book. Or, you can search using key words and phrases on either the **Index** tab or the **Find** tab. All three methods are available in the Help Topics dialog box. To view the dialog box, open the Help menu and choose the Help Topics command.

Using the Contents Tab

The Contents tab of the Help Topics dialog box lets you search cc:Mail's help the same way you would search the table of contents of a book—by subject category. Figure 3.3 shows the Contents tab of the Help Topics dialog box.

Think of each book icon you see on the Contents tab as a major heading in the table of contents. After you select a major heading, you'll see additional subheadings, and eventually, you'll see topics. Topics are represented by pieces of paper containing question marks. When you select a topic, cc:Mail displays the help associated with that topic. Like Guide Me Help, you'll see underlined phrases that you can click for definitions, "for related information" buttons, and so on. To use the Contents tab in the Help Topics dialog box, follow these steps:

1. Double-click any book on-screen to see additional books and help topics (see Figure 3.4).

FIGURE 3.3 Use the Contents tab the same way you would search the table of contents of a book.

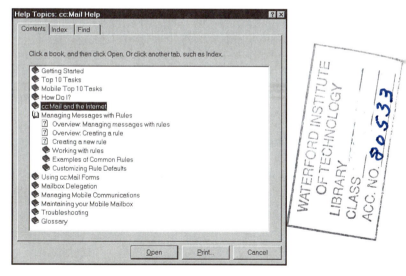

FIGURE 3.4 When you double-click a book, you may see additional books or you may see help topics.

2. Continue to double-click books until you find the topic you want. When you double-click a topic (an image of a paper containing a question mark), cc:Mail displays the actual help information.

3. Click the Close (X) button in a Help topic window when you're finished with the Help feature.

Return to Help Topics dialog box   Most Help windows contain a button bar, below the menu bar, that contains a button titled Help Topics. Click this button to return to the Help Topics dialog box at any time, from anywhere else within Help.

Using the Index Tab

The Index is an alphabetical listing of topics, terms, and phrases you can use to find information and procedures in cc:Mail. Use this tab the same way you would use an index in a book. To use the Index, follow these steps:

1. Open the Help menu and choose the Help Topics command. The Help Topics dialog box appears. Click the Index tab to display the Help Index (see Figure 3.5).

2. You can type a topic in the text box or you can scroll through the list of topics. If you type **send**, for example, you automatically go to the first item in the list that begins with **send**.

3. Select the topic that best describes the help you need and choose the Display button. You can also double-click the desired topic with your mouse. cc:Mail displays one of the following:

   - A Topics Found box from which you choose a specific topic to view and then choose Display.

   - A Help topic providing an overview or listing steps for completing the procedure.

FIGURE 3.5   Search for specific topics by scrolling through the window with your keyboard's down arrow or by typing a topic in the text box.

4. When you're finished, choose one of the following:

- The Close button (X) to exit Help

- The Help Topics button to open the Contents Help screen

- The Go Back button to move to the previous topic viewed

- The Print button to print the topic in the help window

- The Related button, usually found at the bottom of the topic window, to display a list of related topics

USING THE FIND TAB

Find provides a method for narrowing a search of topics in Help. You might, for example, want information about printing. If you type the word **print** in the text box, a list of related words, such as printer, printing, printout, and so on appears. You can let cc:Mail search for all of these topics, or you can narrow the search by typing only the word **printout** or **prints**.

To use Find, follow these steps:

1. Open the Help menu and choose Help Topics. The Help Topics dialog box appears. Choose the Find tab (see Figure 3.6).

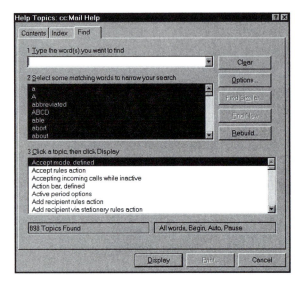

FIGURE 3.6 Find enables you to search for phrases as well as one-word topics.

TIP

Setting Up Find The first time you use the Find tab, cc:Mail displays a dialog box asking you to set up the help database. Choose the Minimize Database Size option button and click the Next button and a second dialog box appears. Choose the Finish button to set up the help database.

2. In the 1 Type the word(s) you want to find text box, type a word, topic, or phrase.

3. In the 2 Select some matching words to narrow your search list, click the topic for which you want to search. To select more than one word, hold the Shift key down as you click the words. You can, alternatively, hold the Ctrl key as you click to select items that are not adjacent.

TIP   **Shortcut**   As you click an individual word in the list, cc:Mail displays related topics in the number 3 Click a topic list box. You can select a topic if you find the one for which you are searching.

4. Choose the topic from the 3 Click a topic, then click Display list box and select the Display button. cc:Mail displays the Help window containing information related to the selected topics.

5. When finished, close the Help window or click Help Topics to redisplay the Help Topics dialog box.

USING HOW DO I?

How Do I? is a list of Help topics that guide you through specific procedures. How Do I? works similarly to any other Help feature in cc:Mail. To use How Do I?, follow these steps:

1. Open the Help menu and choose Help Topics. The Help Topics dialog box appears.

2. Click the Contents tab.

3. Double-click How Do I? to display the list of tasks cc:Mail can walk you through (see Figure 3.7).

FIGURE 3.7   Get help using a list of common tasks.

4. Double-click any book. For example, you can choose Create and Send Messages to see a list of topics related to creating and sending messages.

5. From the list of topics that appears, double-click the topic you want to view.

6. Click the Close button to close the Help window or click the Help Topics button to return to the Help Topics dialog box and choose another topic. To completely close the Help window, click the X in the upper right-hand corner.

In this lesson, you learned to use the Help features: Guide Me, the Contents tab, the Index tab, the Find tab of the Help Topics dialog box, and How Do I?. In the next lesson, you learn to read incoming mail.

READING INCOMING MAIL

In this lesson, you'll learn about the Message pane
and the Preview pane, how to open a message, read your mail, answer
mail, close a message, and preview a message without opening it.

UNDERSTANDING THE MESSAGE PANE

By default, your mailbox appears when you start cc:Mail, displaying the Inbox and any messages in that container. There are other containers in the Mailbox that you'll learn about in following lessons, including the Drafts, Sent Mail, and Trash, among others.

TIP

Identifying Previously Read Messages If you haven't yet read a message, the information about it (sender, date received, and subject) appear in bold blue in the message pane. The same information for messages you have already read appears in plain black text.

cc:Mail provides general information about messages in the message pane: the author, the date the message was sent, and the subject as entered by the sender are all included. You may notice a paper clip next to some messages. The paper clip indicates that the message contains an attachment. You may also notice an exclamation point to the left of the author of some messages (see Figure 4.1). This icon is assigned by the sender of the message and designates a high priority. High priority messages are sent faster over the network.

Attachment An attachment is a document that the sender included in the mail message. These documents may be word processing, presentation, spreadsheet, graphics, or other file types. You can view attachments created with programs you don't have on your computer. Lesson 11 discusses attaching files to messages.

High priority   Attachment

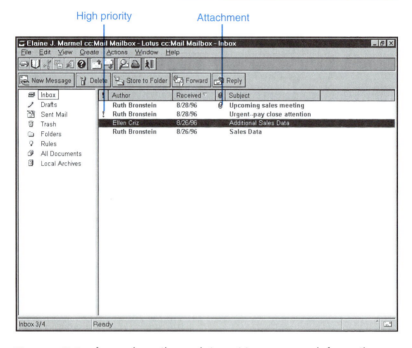

FIGURE 4.1 An exclamation point next to message information indicates the sender put a high priority on the message.

 TIP **Sorting Messages** You can sort the messages in your message pane by author, by date, or by subject. Click the down or up arrow in the Received heading above the message, author, or date to change the sort order. An up arrow displays messages in ascending order (A-to-Z, or oldest first); a down arrow displays messages in descending order (Z-to-A, or newest first).

OPENING YOUR MAIL

You open your mail from the message pane in the Mailbox. After opening and reading your mail, you can reply to it, delete it, print it, or store it. To open your mail and read it, double-click any mail message in the message pane. Figure 4.2 shows an open mail message.

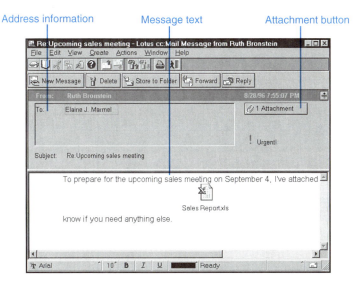

FIGURE 4.2   An open message displays the message text plus additional information.

In the address area, you'll see the name of the sender in the From box, the name(s) of the recipients in the To box, the date and time the message was sent, and the subject of the message.

The attachment button appears only if the message has an attachment, and below the attachment button, you'll see the priority of the message.

At the right and bottom of the message text area are two scroll bars you can use to scroll through the message. If the text of the message appears to run beyond the right edge of the window, you can set page options to force the text to wrap within the boundaries of the window. Follow these steps:

1. Right-click anywhere in the message text area of the open message. cc:Mail displays a shortcut menu.

2. Choose Page Options. You'll see the dialog box shown in Figure 4.3.

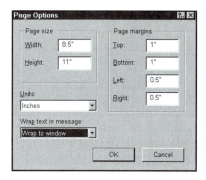

Figure 4.3   From the Page Options dialog box, you can set the parameters cc:Mail will use for the message text.

3. Open the Wrap text in message list box, and choose Wrap to Window.

4. Choose OK. cc:Mail redisplays the open message, and you'll see the text wrapping within the window (see Figure 4.4).

TIP   **Adjust Window Size**   As with any window in cc:Mail, you can minimize, maximize, and restore a mail message window. If the message is maximized (which is the default setting), the Minimize and Restore buttons are located in the menu bar.

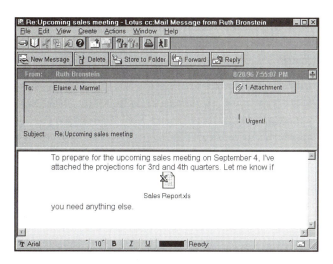

FIGURE 4.4   After setting Page Options to wrap within the message window, you can read text without scrolling to the right.

Saving New Options   When you close the message, cc:Mail will ask if you want to save the new page options you set. If you always want to view message text wrapped to the window, choose Yes.

ANSWERING MAIL

Most of the time, you'll want to answer a message after you read it. You can answer any message quickly and easily. When you choose to answer the message, cc:Mail displays the Reply dialog box. Use the options in the Reply box as follows:

- **Reply to sender.** While the original message may have been sent to multiple recipients, select this option to reply to only the sender of the message.

- **Reply to sender and all recipients.** Select this option to reply to the sender and to all other original recipients of the message.

- **Reply to sender with original message.** Select this option if you want to reply only to the sender of the message and include, in your reply, the original message text.

- **Reply to sender and all recipients with original message.** Select this option to reply to the sender and all other recipients of the message and include, in your reply, the original message text.

To reply to a mail message, follow these steps:

1. Highlight the message to which you want to reply.

2. Click the Reply button on the Action bar. cc:Mail displays the Reply dialog box (see Figure 4.5).

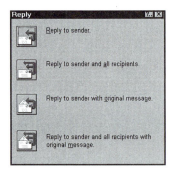

FIGURE 4.5   Use the Reply dialog box to determine who should receive your reply and if the original message text should appear in your reply.

3. Click the icon that identifies the type of reply you want to create. In Figure 4.6, I chose to reply and include the original message text.

 TIP   **Replying without Message Text**   If you choose to reply without including the original message text, the bottom of the Reply window will appear blank.

Send to   Subject containing reference to original message

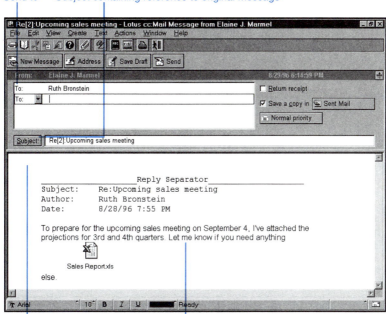

Enter your reply here.   Copy of original message

FIGURE 4.6   When you include the original message text in your reply, it appears in the bottom of the Reply window.

4. Enter your message text in the bottom of the Reply window (above the Reply Separator, if you chose to include the original text).

5. Click the Send Message button in the Action bar to send the message. cc:Mail sends the message, closes the original, and returns you to the Mailbox window.

SAVING A DRAFT

Suppose you're in the middle of replying to a message and you need to stop—maybe you realize you're late for a meeting and you need to leave. You're not yet ready to send the reply message, but you don't want to lose the portion you've already completed.

Click the Save Draft button on the Action bar. cc:Mail will save the reply in the Draft container in the Folder pane. Later, when you have more time, you can reopen the partially completed reply and finish it. Just click the Draft container in the Folder pane, and in the Message pane, you'll see your reply. By default, drafts appear in this pane listed by recipient and date. Double-click the reply to open it.

CLOSING A MESSAGE

You may decide not to reply to a message immediately after reading it. You might want to research the reply, or the message may not require a reply. To close a message, click the Close (X) button in the top-right corner of the message window. Closing a message does not delete it from your mail.

PREVIEWING MESSAGES

Sometimes, you may want to take a quick glance at a message without opening it, to save time. Suppose, for example, that you *think* you know the content of the message and you know that, if you're right, you'll need some time to research before answering. In the meantime, you want to go through the rest of your mail. Use cc:Mail's preview pane to view a message without opening it. Note that, in the Preview pane, you *won't* see icons for attachments; you'll simply see message text.

To view a message in the Preview pane without opening it, follow these steps:

1. In the Message pane, highlight the message you want to view but not open.

2. Open the View menu and choose the Show Preview Pane command. Your Mailbox window changes to look like the one in Figure 4.7.

3. To view another message in the Preview pane, highlight that message in the Message pane.

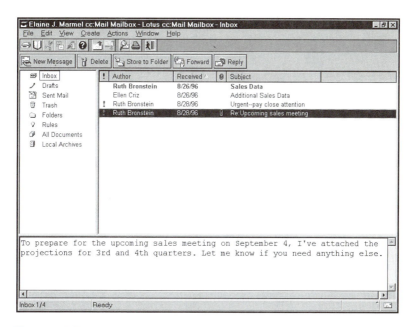

FIGURE 4.7   Use the Preview pane at the bottom of the Mailbox window to take a quick look at the text of a message.

If you want to hide the Preview pane, reopen the View menu and select the Show Preview Pane command again. Notice that, when the Preview pane is visible in the Mailbox window, a check appears to the left of the command on the View menu. Choosing the command again removes the check and hides the Preview pane.

UPDATING THE INBOX

cc:Mail doesn't automatically display new mail while you're working in the Inbox. You can at any time, however, *refresh* the Inbox so that you can see new mail. To refresh the Inbox, press F9. You can also choose Refresh from the View menu. A dialog box will notify you of new messages, and any new messages will appear in the list.

In this lesson, you learned to open a message, read your mail, answer mail, save a draft of a reply, close a message, preview mail, and update the Inbox. In the next lesson, you'll learn to print, delete, save, and forward mail.

5 LESSON

MANAGING INCOMING MAIL

In this lesson, you'll learn how to forward, print, and delete mail messages as well as how to create folders, and save mail to those folders.

FORWARDING MAIL

You can forward any message you receive to one or more people on your network or to one or more groups. When forwarding a message, you can add your own comments to the message or you can forward the message without making any changes.

ADDING TEXT TO A FORWARDED MESSAGE

To add text to a message you want to forward, start by opening the message. Follow these steps:

1. In the Message pane, open the message you want to forward.

2. Click the Forward Message button on the Action bar. The Forward dialog box appears (see Figure 5.1).

FIGURE 5.1   Decide whether to forward the history with the message.

3. Choose whether to Retain forwarding history. If you do, cc:Mail will include a separator line at the top of the message and send, along the with the text of the message, the subject, author, and date of the message.

4. Choose OK. In the space above the separator line, enter your message.

5. In the To box, enter the name of the person you want to forward the message to. Be sure to use their cc:Mail name as described by the system administrator; this may mean typing the last name first.

TIP   **Internet addresses**   You can send mail to Internet addresses using cc:Mail if you have the Internet address of the person to whom you want to send mail. You'll learn more about addressing messages in Lesson 6.

6. Click the Send button on the Action bar and cc:Mail sends the message to the address you've entered.

FORWARDING A MESSAGE WITHOUT ADDING TEXT

If you don't want to add text to a message you plan to forward, then you don't need to open the message to forward it. Follow these steps:

1. In the Message pane of the Mailbox window, highlight the message you want to forward.

2. Click the Forward button on the Action bar. The Forward Recipients dialog box appears (see Figure 5.2).

3. Type the name of the person to whom you want to forward the message or select the person from the list. Click To-> to add a person to the list of recipients.

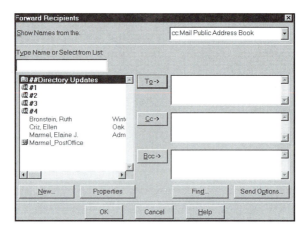

FIGURE 5.2   Use this dialog box to identify recipients of a message you want to forward from the Mailbox window.

Wondering About Those Icons?   The numbered icons in the list represent mailing lists; you'll learn more about mailing lists in Lesson 6.

4. (Optional) To send a carbon copy, type another name or select another person from the list and choose Cc->. To send a blind carbon copy, choose Bcc->.

5. Choose OK. cc:Mail displays the Forward dialog box.

6. Choose whether to Retain forwarding history and choose Send.

CANCELING A MESSAGE

You may begin a new message, a reply to a message, or forward a message and then change your mind about sending the message. You can cancel any open message without sending it or saving it.

To cancel a message, follow these steps:

1. In the open message window, click the Close button (X) or press the Esc key. The Modified Message dialog box appears (see Figure 5.3).

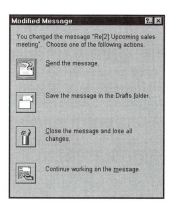

FIGURE 5.3 If you change your mind while working on a message, use this dialog box to decide what to do with the message you started.

2. In the dialog box, choose one of the following buttons:

- Send the message.
- Save the message in the Drafts folder.
- Close the message and lose all changes.
- Continue working on the message.

TIP

Save Draft?   Remember, you can, as an alternative to canceling the message, choose the Save Draft button on the Action bar in the Message window. cc:Mail will save your message to the Drafts container in the Folder pane of the Mailbox window and you can open, edit, or send it later. To open a draft, click the Drafts folder; then double-click the message to open it. After opening a Draft message, you can send it, print it, move it, and otherwise treat it like any other message.

PRINTING A MESSAGE

You can print a message from the Message pane of the Mailbox window or from an open message window. Depending on where you are when you choose to print, various options appear in the Print Options dialog box.

PRINTING AN OPEN MESSAGE

Figure 5.4 shows the Print Header Options dialog box you see if you choose to print an open message from the Message window.

FIGURE 5.4   The Print Header Options dialog box offers printing options for an open message.

To print an open message, follow these steps:

1. Open the message you want to print.

2. Click the Print List, Item, or Message SmartIcon. The Print Header Options dialog box appears.

TIP   **Are You a Keyboard Person?**   Press Ctrl+P or choose File, Print to display the Print Options.

3. Choose options for printing (see Table 5.1).

4. Choose OK. cc:Mail displays the Print dialog box, which shows the printer cc:Mail will use when it prints the message.

5. Choose OK. cc:Mail prints the message, including the header options you specified.

Table 5.1 describes the options in this Print Options dialog box.

TABLE 5.1 PRINTING OPTIONS FOR THE MESSAGE WINDOW

OPTION	DESCRIPTION
None	Prints only the message text.
Partial	Prints the message text and any of the following, depending on what you choose: Author, Subject, Date/Time the message was sent, Recipients, and Priority.
Full	Prints all of the choices available in the Partial option. In addition, you can include forwarding history and you can instruct cc:Mail to print each recipient's name on a separate line.

 TIP **Identify What You're Printing** Place a check in the Header Text check box and type a phrase that you want to appear at the top of the printout. You might want to include, in the phrase, the printing options you used or the subject of the message. This box defaults to the product name; to insert your own text, highlight the existing text string and type your replacement text.

PRINTING AN UNOPENED MESSAGE

Figure 5.5 shows the Print Options dialog box you see when you choose to print an unopened message from the Message pane of the Mailbox window.

FIGURE 5.5   Your printing options change when you choose to print from the Mailbox window.

To print an unopened message, follow these steps:

1. Click the Print List, Item, or Message SmartIcon. The Print Options dialog box appears.

2. Choose from the following printing options:

   - **Message List**   Prints the list of messages in the Message pane of the Mailbox window.

   - **Message(s) with all attachments**   Prints the selected message(s) and the icon of any attachments associated with the e-mail message. (To print the attachment itself, unless it's plain text, would require opening the attachment.)

3. Choose OK. cc:Mail prints the selected messages and/or attachment icons.

DELETING A MESSAGE

Deleting messages in cc:Mail is the first step in the process of removing them entirely from your hard disk. To delete a message, place it in the Trash container (Deleted Items) in the Folders pane. cc:Mail keeps track of messages in the Trash container and either deletes them for you at a pre-specified time or waits for you to empty the Trash. Using the Trash container provides you with a double-check; a deleted message is retained for a time, giving you the chance to change your mind about deleting it.

The frequency with which cc:Mail deletes messages in the Trash container depends on the settings you choose. See Lesson 9 for information about customizing the Trash settings.

Wait! When a deleted message is finally emptied from the Trash, you cannot retrieve the message. Do not delete messages or allow them to be automatically emptied from the Trash unless you are positive you no longer want them. If you change your mind and want to keep a message you placed in the Trash, drag the message from the Trash to an appropriate folder.

To move a message to the Trash so that cc:Mail will delete it, follow these steps:

1. Select the message in the Message pane of the Mailbox window.

2. Press the Delete key. A confirmation dialog box appears, asking if you want to delete the message. You can also click the Delete button.

3. Choose OK to confirm the deletion.

Delete Multiple Messages You can select more than one message for deletion by holding the Shift or the Ctrl key as you click on each message to be deleted; then press the Delete key and confirm the deletion. The Shift key allows you to select contiguous messages, the Ctrl key allows you to choose non-contiguous messages.

Mouse Person? Select the message(s) you want to delete and drag them to the Trash container in the Folder pane. When cc:Mail displays the Move confirmation dialog box, choose OK.

Regardless of which method you use to get messages into the Trash container (the mouse or the keyboard), cc:Mail won't delete them until the time specified in your settings or unless you tell cc:Mail to empty the trash. To tell cc:Mail to empty the trash, open the Actions menu and choose the Empty Trash command. You can also click the Empty Trash button. cc:Mail displays a confirmation message that indicates you are permanently deleting the message(s) from your system. Choose OK, and cc:Mail empties the trash.

CREATING A FOLDER

To help you keep your mail messages organized, you can create folders and place the messages in them. A folder helps you group related messages together.

 Folder A folder is another word for a directory. When you create a folder, you're adding a directory to the drive on which you plan to store your messages.

To create a folder, follow these steps:

   1. Open the Create menu and choose the Folder command. cc:Mail displays the Create New Folder dialog box (see Figure 5.6).

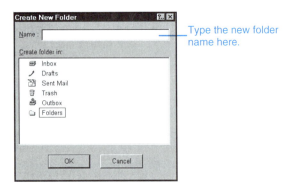

Type the new folder name here.

FIGURE 5.6   Enter a name and choose a container to complete the folder creation.

2. Enter the name for the new folder.

3. Choose OK when you are done. cc:Mail creates the new folder and places it inside the Folders container.

 What about the Other Containers? Although you see the other containers in the dialog box, you cannot create a new folder and place it inside any container except the Folders container.

You'll notice a right-pointing arrow next to a container in the Folder pane in which you placed the new folder. If you double-click the **Folders** container, cc:Mail changes the arrow to a down-pointing arrow and expands the view to show you all the folders inside that container. You can also click the arrow itself, and this turns it down so that you can see the folders inside the container. To collapse this view, click the arrow again, and it turns back up.

Storing Mail in a Folder

You can clean out your Inbox by moving messages to folders. Any message you move from the Inbox to a folder is available for later reference or use. You can open, print, forward, and otherwise manipulate messages from any folder.

 Deciding Where to Store You cannot simply save a message to the Folders container; you must save a message to a folder you've created within the Folders container.

To save mail to a folder, follow these steps:

1. Expand the Folders container so that you can see all the folders inside it.

2. Click a message you want to move to a folder, and drag it to the appropriate location.

Mouse Pointer Shapes!   As you drag, the mouse pointer changes shapes. If the pointer becomes a black circle with a line crossed through it, you cannot move the message to the selected container. Alternatively, if the pointer becomes an arrow with a dotted rectangle attached, you can move the message to the selected container.

3. You can release the mouse button when you see a solid rectangle outlining the folder in which you want to place the message. cc:Mail displays the confirmation Move dialog box that asks you if you want to move the message to the folder.

TIP   **Move Multiple Messages**   You can move more than one message at a time by holding the Shift or the Ctrl key as you click on each message you want to move. The Shift key allows you to choose contiguous messages, the Ctrl key allows you to choose non-contiguous messages. Then drag all of the selected messages to the appropriate folder.

4. Choose OK to complete the move.

You can open the folder containing the moved messages by double-clicking the folder.

In this lesson, you learned to forward, print and delete mail messages, to create folders, and to save mail to folders. In the next lesson, you will learn to work with addresses.

UNDERSTANDING ADDRESSES AND MAILING LISTS

6

In this lesson, you'll learn about addresses, you'll view and use the cc:Mail Public Address Book, and you'll use public and personal mailing lists.

WORKING IN THE ADDRESS WINDOW

When you write a new cc:Mail message to send to someone, you must put an address on it so that it will be directed to the person you intend to receive it. People are assigned addresses by the cc:Mail administrator. Typically, the cc:Mail administrator manages one post office and all the users of that post office. The post office contains a mailbox for each user and the mailbox holds incoming mail for the user.

In addition to the users attached to your local post office, you can also send mail to users belonging to other cc:Mail post offices attached to your network. You use the address books and mailing lists to send mail to other cc:Mail users. Or, you can type their addresses directly into the TO box as you prepare the message.

Address Books   cc:Mail contains two types of address books: a public address book that shows all the entries in your post office, and a personal address book that stores e-mail addresses that you intend to use but might or might not appear in your post office.

Mailing Lists   cc:Mail uses two types of mailing lists: public and personal. The public lists are created by the cc:Mail administrator; you create and maintain your own personal mailing lists.

You can work with addresses in two places in cc:Mail: in the Address Book dialog box and in the Address Book window. You use the Address Book dialog box to address messages while you create them. To manage addresses, you use the Address Book window.

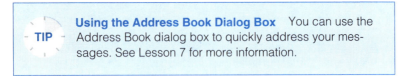

TIP   **Using the Address Book Dialog Box**   You can use the Address Book dialog box to quickly address your messages. See Lesson 7 for more information.

cc:Mail includes an Address Book window from which you can obtain various addresses. Addresses can be obtained from both your local post office and other post offices, as well as remote users and even from the Internet, if they've been added to your address book. To open the Address Book window, open the Window menu and choose Address Book. Figure 6.1 shows a sample address book window.

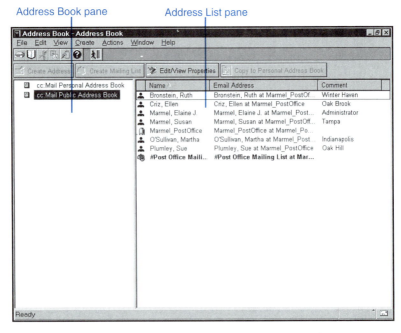

FIGURE 6.1   Use the Address Book window to view the contents of the Public Address Book and manage the contents of your Personal Address Book.

USING THE ADDRESS BOOK PANE

Similar to the Mailbox window, the Address Book window presents a pane on the left in which Address Book containers appear. The Address Book pane includes two address containers:

- **Personal Address Book**   Your personal address book entries, usually consisting of individuals or mailing lists to which you often send e-mail.

- **Public Address Book**   A container that includes all users, mailing lists, post offices, gateways, and bulletin boards in your organization. The Public Address Book displays the name, address, and comments for each entry.

Click either of these two Address Book containers in the Address Book pane, and the contents will appear in the Address List Pane of the Address Book window.

Gateway   A gateway is a bridge, of sorts, that enables you to travel outside the confines of your local network. For example, you can use a gateway to send and receive mail using the Internet.

Bulletin Board   A bulletin board is a location, created by the administrator, where you can post and read public messages. For example, your company might have a "For Sale" bulletin board. See Lesson 14 for more information.

USING THE ADDRESS LIST PANE

The Address List pane of the Address Book window displays the names and other information included in the selected container (see Figure 6.2).

Following is a description of each part of an address, as shown in the figure:

- **Type**   An icon that indicates whether the item is a person, post office, mailing list, or gateway.

- **Name**   A friendly name for the person, post office, mailing list or gateway.

- **Email Address**   The address used by cc:Mail to distribute mail to the person, post office, mailing list, bulletin board, or gateway.

- **Comment**   Usually a title, description, or location of the person, post office, or gateway, entered by the cc:Mail administrator to help you identify the user.

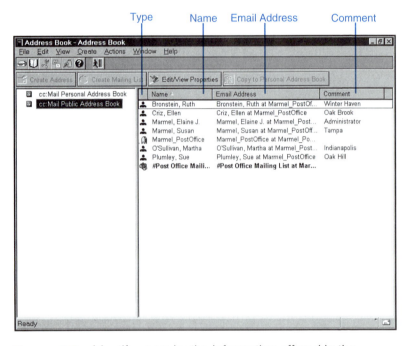

FIGURE 6.2   Identify users by the information offered in the Address List pane.

 Friendly Name   Friendly names are shortcuts you can use to call up the recipient's full e-mail address. You can think of them as nicknames for e-mail addresses.

 # Symbols   In addition to the icon identifying bulletin boards and mailing lists, each mailing list in the Public Address Book is preceded with a single pound sign (#).

In addition to the information you see displayed by default in the Address List pane, you can customize the pane to also display the information listed in Table 6.1.

TABLE 6.1   INFORMATION YOU CAN DISPLAY IN THE ADDRESS LIST PANE

ITEM	MEANING
First Name	The person's first name
Initials	The person's initials
Last Name	The person's last name
ASCII Name	A version of the user's name that can be displayed in e-mail systems that use 7-bit (128-character) ASCII.
MHS Common Name	A name that can be used in the message header, which includes information about the message such as the author, the subject, the recipients, etc.
Transmittable Name	A name that cannot be altered by another user
Send Rich Text	Indicates whether a recipient's e-mail system supports rich text formatting
Address Type	The type of the mail service provider, such as CCMAIL
Last Logged In	The date and time the person last logged on to cc:Mail

ASCII   ASCII stands for American Standard Code for Information Interchange. It's a worldwide standard for the codes used by computers to represent common numbers and letters.

Rich Text   Formatting of text that includes multiple fonts, margin settings, indents, and graphics. cc:Mail allows you to use rich text.

To add any of these items to the Address List pane, open the View menu and choose the Design List View command. You'll see the Folder List View dialog box shown in Figure 6.3.

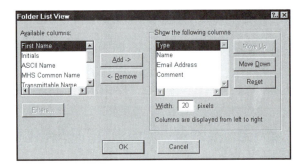

FIGURE 6.3   Use this dialog box to add columns to the Address List pane.

Take any of the following actions, and click the OK button when you finish:

- To add a column, highlight it in the Available columns list box and click the Add button.

- To remove a column, highlight it in the Show the Following Columns list box and click the Remove button.

- To reorder the columns in the Address List pane, use the Show the Following Columns list box. Highlight the item you want to move and click either the Move Up button or the Move Down button. Click the buttons repeatedly to move items further up or down in the list.

• To change the amount of space allocated to any column, use the Width text box.

• To restore the original appearance of the columns, click Reset.

UNDERSTANDING THE PUBLIC ADDRESS BOOK

The Public Address Book lists all users, post offices, mailing lists and gateways available to you through cc:Mail. You cannot add or delete any names from the Public Address book or from any public mailing list. Only the cc:Mail administrator can do that.

You can view more information about any user, post office, or gateway in any of the containers by clicking the Edit/View Properties button on the Action bar or by double-clicking the name in the Address List pane. The Properties dialog box for the selected item appears (see Figure 6.4).

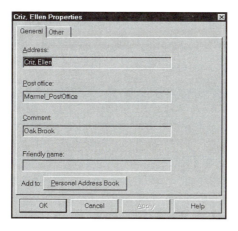

FIGURE 6.4 From this dialog box, you can identify information about the selected person.

The information on the General tab of the Properties dialog box includes the name, Email address, any comments the cc:Mail administrator added, and the friendly name, if any, for the person. The Other tab provides a place to include additional comments. Choose OK to close the Properties dialog box and save changes you make.

COPYING ADDRESSES FROM THE PUBLIC TO THE PERSONAL ADDRESS BOOK

Suppose you see someone in the Public Address Book whose address you'd like to place in your Personal Address Book. You can easily copy the address from the Public Address Book to your Personal Address Book.

1. In the Address List pane, highlight the name of the person whose address you want to copy.

2. Click the Copy to Personal Address Book button on the Action bar. cc:Mail copies the name.

Check the Personal Address Book container by clicking it once in the Address Book pane. You'll see an entry, in the Address List pane, for the person whose e-mail address you copied.

TIP   **Creating a Friendly Name**   Once you copy an address into your Personal Address Book, you can assign that person a "friendly name" similar to a nickname you might use for that person. When you assign a friendly name to someone, it will appear under the Name column in your address book. To create a friendly name, select the person and click the Edit/View Properties button on the Action bar. In the Properties dialog box, click in the Friendly Name box and type the name.

CREATING A PERSONAL MAILING LIST

By default, there are no personal mailing lists in the cc:Mail Address Book window until you create your own. You can add names to a personal mailing list during or after the creation of the mailing list. In this section, we'll walk through the steps of creating the mailing list without adding members to it. In the next section, you'll learn how to add (or delete) names to a mailing list.

To create a personal mailing list, follow these steps:

1. Click the Personal Address Book container in the Address Book pane.

2. Click the Create Mailing List button on the Action bar or open the Create menu and choose the Mailing List command. cc:Mail displays the New cc:Mail Mailing List Properties dialog box (see Figure 6.5).

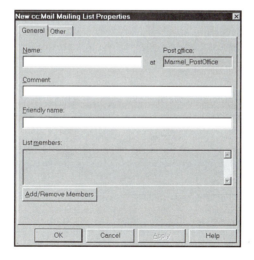

FIGURE 6.5   Choose the names you want to add to your personal mailing list.

3. In the Name box, enter a name for the mailing list.

4. (Optional) Enter a Comment and a Friendly Name for the Mailing List using the respective boxes. If you need more room for your comment, click the Other tab and place the comment there.

5. Choose OK.

ADDING AND DELETING ADDRESSES IN A PERSONAL MAIL LIST

I mentioned, in the previous section, that you can add members to your mailing list as you create it. It is likely, however, that you will need to modify a mailing list sometime after you create it—either to add or remove names from the list.

To change the contents of a personal mailing list, follow these steps:

1. Click the Personal Address Book container in the Address Book pane.

2. In the Address List pane, double-click the mailing list you want to modify.

3. To add a member to or remove a member from your mailing list, click the Add/Remove Members button. You'll see the Mailing List dialog box shown in Figure 6.6.

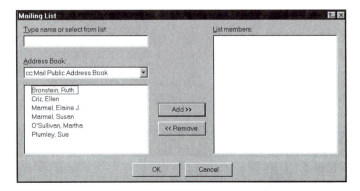

FIGURE 6.6 Use this dialog box to change the recipients included in a mailing list.

4. Take one of the following actions:

- To add a name, type the name you want to add or select it from the list. Click Add. If you add a name to a mailing list that wasn't in your Personal Address Book, cc:Mail will automatically add the name to both the mailing list and your Personal Address Book.

- To delete a name, select it from the List Members box(on the right side of the dialog box) and choose the Remove button.

5. Choose OK.

Who's in the Mailing List? To view the names in a personal mailing list, double-click the mailing list name in the Address List pane to display the mailing list's Properties dialog box. You'll see the list of members toward the bottom of the box.

Rename or Delete List You can rename your private mailing list at any time by reopening the Properties dialog box and changing the name. To delete a mailing list, highlight it in the Address List pane and press the Del key. cc:Mail displays the Delete confirmation dialog box; choose OK to delete the list.

In this lesson, you learned about the Address window in cc:Mail and you learned to view and understand the contents of the Public Address Book and the Personal Address Book. You also learned to copy addresses from the Public Address Book to your Personal Address Book and create and alter personal mailing lists. In the next lesson, you'll learn how to send mail.

7 Lesson SENDING MAIL

In this lesson, you'll learn to create a mail message, to address the message, to use carbon copies and blind carbon copies, and to send the message.

CREATING A MESSAGE

You create a new message in the Mailbox window. When you create a new message, you'll notice the familiar title bar, menu bar, SmartIcons, and Action bar, along with some new areas (see Figure 7.1).

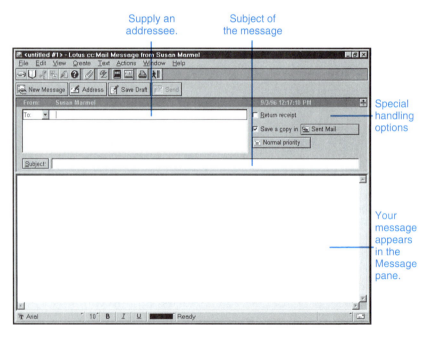

Supply an addressee.

Subject of the message

Special handling options

Your message appears in the Message pane.

FIGURE 7.1 Use the Message window to create a message.

To display the Message window and create a message, click the
New Message button on the Action bar; alternatively, press
Ctrl+M. To complete the message, you'll need to enter an address,
subject, and message text. You may also want to choose some
special handling options for the message before sending it.

Addressing a Message

So you're sure to get the names and addresses right, it is best if
you use your address book to help you address messages. You can
choose an address from the Address Message dialog box. You can
send a message to any user or group in the address list.

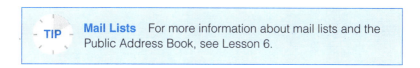

> **TIP**   **Mail Lists**   For more information about mail lists and the
> Public Address Book, see Lesson 6.

To address a newly created message, follow these steps:

1. Click the Address button on the Action bar. The Address
    Book dialog box appears (see Figure 7.2)

Choose an
Address Book.

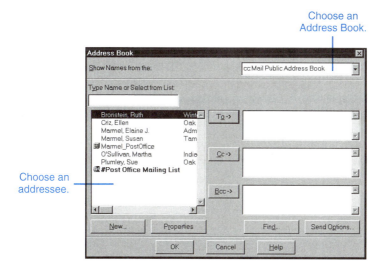

Choose an
addressee.

Figure 7.2   Use this dialog box to address the message.

2. Open the list box at the top of the Address Book dialog box and choose an Address Book to use either the Public Address Book or your Personal Address Book.

3. From the list on the left side of the Address Book dialog box, choose the mailing list or person to whom you want to send the message.

4. Choose one of the following buttons:

   • To->   Indicates the primary mailing list, post office or person to whom the message will be sent.

   • Cc->   Indicates that a carbon copy of the message will be sent to the selected person, mailing list, or post office.

   • Bcc->   Indicates that a blind carbon copy will be sent to the selected person, mailing list, or post office.

Blind Copy   When you send a blind carbon copy, cc:Mail sends the copy to the recipient without adding the recipient's name to the list that others will see. Blind carbon copies are available in case you don't want your recipients to know everyone to whom you have sent a copy.

5. Repeat steps 3 and 4 until you've selected all recipients of the message.

6. Choose OK. cc:Mail returns to the Message window with the addresses listed.

TIP

Fax Address   If your post office has an optional cc:Fax gateway, you can send a message to any fax number. See your cc:Mail administrator for the gateway name and for details about addressing the fax.

ENTERING A SUBJECT

You can type a subject into the Subject text box. Your subject can be any combination of text, numbers, or other characters; generally, you try to use a subject the recipient can quickly relate to.

As an alternative to typing the subject, you can click the Subject button and choose from a preset subject to save time. To enter a subject using this method, follow these steps:

1. In the Message window, click the Subject button. The Subjects dialog box appears (see Figure 7.3).

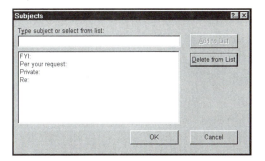

FIGURE 7.3   Assign a subject to your message.

TIP   **Moving from Box to Box**   You can quickly move from box to box by pressing the Tab key.

2. In the Type Subject or Select From List text box, enter a subject of your own; alternatively, select a subject heading from the list.

3. Choose OK when you are done. cc:Mail returns to the Message window with the subject entered in the appropriate place.

4. To expand upon the subject you selected from the Subjects dialog box, click at the end of the text appearing in the Subject text box and enter additional text, such as FYI: Sales Reports.

Modifying the Available Subjects   To add a frequently used subject to the list in the Subjects dialog box, enter the subject in the Type Subject or Select from List text box, and then choose the Add to List button. To delete a subject from the list, highlight the subject and click the Delete from List button.

ENTERING AND FORMATTING THE MESSAGE

You enter the message in the Message window, which is the large white box below the subject. Enter text as you would in any application, using the **Backspace** and **Delete** keys to correct mistakes, pressing **Enter** to start a new paragraph, the **Tab** key to indent text, and so on. Since cc:Mail supports rich text formatting, you can change the font, font size, and font color; or you can apply bold, italics, or underline to any portion of your message. Use the buttons on the status bar of the Message window (see Figure 7.4).

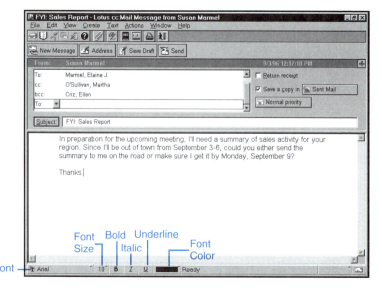

FIGURE 7.4   Use the status bar to apply formatting to portions of your message text.

Formatting if you're sending your message over the Internet, any formatting will disappear. And, in most cases, you lose any formatting if your message goes through a gateway to another mail system.

 If you're more comfortable making choices from boxes, click the Text Properties SmartIcon to display the Text Properties InfoBox (see Figure 7.5).

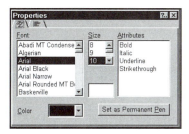

Figure 7.5 You can also change text formatting from the Text Properties InfoBox.

You can apply text formatting to your message as you type or after you've typed. Suppose you want to add formatting while you type. Follow these steps:

1. When you reach the word where you want the formatting to start, click the button on the status bar to begin applying that formatting.

2. Type.

3. When you reach the word where the formatting should end, click the formatting button a second time.

Now let's suppose you want to apply formatting after you've typed your message. Follow these steps:

1. Select the text you want to format by clicking the left mouse button at the beginning of the text and dragging the mouse I-beam to the end of the text.

2. Click the appropriate button on the status bar or use the Text Properties SmartIcon to open the Text Properties InfoBox and apply formatting.

Want to Permanently Change the Font? Change the font, font size, attributes, and color, and then click the **Set as Permanent Pen** button.

To make changes to the margins and alignment of the message, follow these steps:

1. Place the insertion point in the paragraph where you want the new margins and/or alignment to begin.

 2. Click the Text Properties SmartIcon to open the Text Properties InfoBox.

3. Click the Margins and Alignment tab (see Figure 7.6).

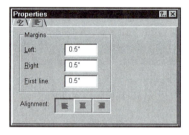

FIGURE 7.6 Change the margins and/or alignment of your message.

4. Make either of the following changes and then press Enter:

- Enter new measurements in the Left and Right text boxes; the numbers, or measurements, represent characters in the current font. To create a hanging indent, enter a smaller value in the First Line text box than the value you enter in the Left text box.

- Choose an alignment.

Closing an InfoBox To close an InfoBox, click the X in the upper-right corner of the InfoBox.

TIP

Can't Make Up Your Mind? If you want to try out different combinations of text formatting, use the Text Properties InfoBox, but don't close it after each change; just double-click its title bar to shrink it so that all you see is the title bar. Shrinking the Infobox will allow you to see the alterations to your text. Double-click the title bar again to return the Text Properties InfoBox to its original size.

CHECKING SPELLING

You can check the spelling in your message text to guarantee that you send professional messages to your colleagues. The spelling checker in cc:Mail works similarly to spelling checkers in most word processing programs. The Spell Check dialog box displays any words not found in the program's "dictionary." You can choose to ignore the misspelling cc:Mail finds, replace the word with the correct spelling, or add the word to the dictionary so that the spell checker won't question it again. But remember, spell checking doesn't replace proofreading, because spell checking won't catch missing words or inappropriate word choices (that is, spell checking will allow "patch" even though you meant "path").

Dictionary cc:Mail includes a dictionary of common words, excluding many technical terms, names, cities, jargon, and so on; therefore, even some correctly spelled words may be questioned.

Figure 7.7 shows the Spell Check dialog box and Table 7.1 describes the options in the dialog box.

FIGURE 7.7   Use the Spell Check dialog box to correct your spelling.

TABLE 7.1   SPELL CHECK OPTIONS

OPTION	DESCRIPTION
Change to	Enter the correct spelling in this text box; alternatively, select the correctly spelled word from the Suggestions list, and it appears in this text box.
Suggestions	Choose from a list of alternatives.
Ignore	Disregard only this instance of the misspelled word and continue spell checking.
Ignore All	Disregard all instances of the misspelled word in this document and continue checking.
Change	Correct only this one instance of the misspelled word and continue checking.
Change All	Correct all instances of the misspelled word in this document and continue checking.
Add	Add this word to the dictionary so it will not be questioned again and continue checking.
Cancel	Cancel the spelling check.

Canceling Spell Checking If cc:Mail found a misspelled word when you chose to cancel, you'd see a message indicating that a spelling error was found; you would then be asked if you want to continue. In this case, "continue" means "continue canceling." Choose OK to cancel spell checking.

To check the spelling in your message, follow these steps:

1. Position the insertion point at the beginning of the message text and click the Spell Check SmartIcon.

Started in the Wrong Place? As you just discovered, the location of the insertion point does matter. If the insertion point rests in the middle of a word, Spell Check assumes *that* position is the beginning of the message and reports a misspelled word. Cancel Spell Checking and start again.

2. Make the appropriate selections in the Spell Check dialog box, referring to Table 7.1 when necessary.

3. When it is finished, cc:Mail displays a dialog box informing you the spell check is complete. Choose OK to close the message box and the Spell Check dialog box.

SETTING SPECIAL HANDLING OPTIONS

Before you send a message, you may want to set options for special handling of your message. Immediately next to the area where recipients appear in the Message window, you can set the following special handling options:

- **Return receipt** Placing a check in this box tells cc:Mail to notify you when the recipient receives your message.

- **Save a copy in**   Placing a check in this box tells cc:Mail to save a copy of the message in the folder you specify. Click the check box, and then click the button to the right of it to choose a folder—you'll see a list of potential locations for the message.

- **Priority**   By default, cc:Mail sets the priority for new mail messages to Normal. By clicking this button, you can change the priority to Urgent or Low Priority. You can click the button repeatedly to cycle through the available priority options. The priority indicates to the recipient how important you think the message is. In addition, it can affect the speed with which your message is delivered, depending on the setup of your post office. Check with your administrator.

COMPLETING THE MESSAGE

When you're ready to send the message, you can quickly and easily send it on its way. Just click the Send button on the Action bar. You'll see a confirmation dialog box before cc:Mail sends your message.

But, you may not be ready to send at the time you need to close the message; perhaps you need to go to a meeting, and you want to finish the message later. In that case, you might want to cancel the message or perhaps save the message as a draft. Or, maybe you want a hard copy of the message before you send it—so you want to print the message.

 TIP   **Attachments**   You might also want to attach a file, import, or export text by using the second, or attachment, pane of the Message window. See Lessons 11 and 12 for more information.

SAVING A DRAFT

To save a copy of your message to the Drafts folder, click the Save Draft button on the Action bar. You'll see no confirmation message, but cc:Mail will close the Message window and redisplay the cc:Mail window. You'll find a copy of your message in the Drafts folder if you click it in the Folder pane.

PRINTING A MESSAGE

To print the message, click the Print SmartIcon. You'll see the Print Header Options dialog box. Use Table 7.2 to determine the options you want to set. When you finish selecting options, click OK.

TABLE 7.2   PRINTING OPTIONS FOR THE MESSAGE WINDOW

OPTION	DESCRIPTION
None	Prints only the message text.
Partial	Prints the message text and any of the following, depending on what you choose: Author, Subject, Date/Time the message was sent, Recipients, and Priority.
Full	Prints all of the choices available in the Partial option. In addition, you can include forwarding history and you can instruct cc:Mail to print each recipient's name on a separate line.
Header Text	Identifies what you're printing. Place a check in the box and type a phrase that you want to appear at the top of the printout.

CLOSING THE MESSAGE WITHOUT SAVING IT

Suppose you decide that you don't want to send the message after all and you know you won't want to ever send it. In fact, you just want to quit working on it. Press the Esc key to display the Modified Message dialog box (see Figure 7.8).

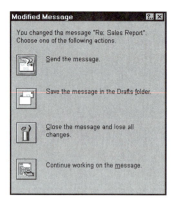

FIGURE 7.8   Use the Modified Message dialog box to cancel a message.

    TIP   **One Stop Shopping**   Using the Modified Message dialog box, you can do much more than simply delete a message. You can quickly choose to send the message, save the message as a draft, or keep working on the message.

Choose from one of the following options:

- Send the Message.   The message is sent to the recipients listed.

- Save the message in the Drafts folder.   cc:Mail places a copy of the message in the Drafts folder for you to review, delete, or send later.

- Close the message and lose all changes.   Cancels the message completely.

- Continue working on the message.   Closes the dialog box and returns to the message window so that you can finish the message.

SAVING THE MESSAGE AS A FILE

You might want to save the message as a file for later use or referral. Remember, however, saving a message in this manner saves only the text of the message, not the address information; this method of saving a message is especially useful when you need the message text in another program. In addition, the saved file is in cc:Mail message format, so you can open it, edit it, print it, or send it later. To save a message, follow these steps:

1. Choose File, Save As File. The Save As dialog box appears (see Figure 7.9).

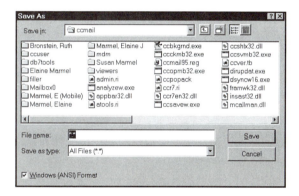

FIGURE 7.9   Use this dialog box to save a message to a file for later use.

2. From the Save in list box, select the folder to which you want to save the message.

3. In the File name text box, type a name for the file.

4. You can also choose an alternate location for the file at this point, by using the save dialogue box toolbar or clicking on another folder in the display.

5. Click Save.

In this lesson, you learned to create a mail message, address the message, use copies and blind copies, and send the message. In the next lesson, you'll learn to set mail options.

LESSON 8

SETTING MESSAGE OPTIONS

In this lesson, you'll learn to set mail options, such as the default message priority, the message background, and pen colors.

SETTING SPECIAL HANDLING OPTIONS

You can set special handling options when you create a new message by modifying the default choices for special handling in the New Message window (see Figure 8.1).

Click here to select a priority level for your message.

Check here to save a copy of the message in your Sent Mail folder.

Check here to request a receipt notification message.

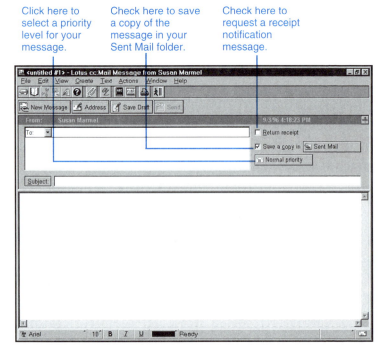

FIGURE 8.1   Set options before sending your message.

cc:Mail provides the following options for you to consider before sending your new message:

- **Return receipt**   Select this option by displaying a **checkmark** in the check box and you will be notified when the message you sent is received by the recipient. For example, if you send a message to a co-worker on the morning of March 4, 1996 with the subject **Reorganization**, when the recipient opens your message, cc:Mail automatically sends you back a message with a subject line that reads **Receipt of 3/4/96 9:12 AM message** and a message body that reads **Re: Reorganization**.

- **Save a copy in**   When this option is checked, cc:Mail puts a copy of the message in a folder you select. The default folder is the Sent Mail folder.

- **Priority**   Select from Normal, Low, or Urgent priority. Setting priority informs the recipient of the importance of the message and may also determine how quickly the message is delivered, depending on how your post office is set up. Ask your administrator for details.

When you change any of these options and then send the message, cc:Mail asks if you want to save the changes so that cc:Mail will use those options by default for all future messages.

SETTING DEFAULT OPTIONS FOR NEW MESSAGES

Message options are user preferences you can change to suit your specific needs. For new messages you create, you can set defaults for which Address Book (Public or Personal) you will use, the color of message text, and so on. Table 8.1 describes the options you can set for working in the New Message window.

TABLE 8.1   MESSAGE OPTIONS

OPTION	DESCRIPTION
Start in	Choose from this list box to determine where cc:Mail starts (and what you see) when you create a new message. For example, if you choose Addressing Dialog, cc:Mail opens the New Message window and displays the Address Book dialog box.
Address	From this list box, choose the recipient whose address you want to appear first in the Message Window's Address pane: the main recipient (To), the carbon copy recipients (CC), or the blind carbon copy recipients (BCC).
Priority	Set the default priority to Normal, Urgent, or Low.
Enable Save Copy	Check this box to automatically save a copy of your messages to the folder of your choice.
Request receipt	Check this box to automatically request a receipt notification on every message.
Automatic spell check	Check this box to have cc:Mail automatically check the spelling of messages when you send them.
Quick addressing	Check this box if you want to type part of a recipient's name and have cc:Mail check an Address Book and fill in the rest of the name and address. If you mark this box, you must also select the address book cc:Mail will check.
Default text color	Use this list box to select a default pen color for the Message Text area of the Message Window.

User Preferences User preferences are options you can change to make your work easier in cc:Mail. The cc:Mail program sets defaults for user preferences to the most common settings; you do not have to change any of these settings, but you can, if you want.

 TIP **User Preferences** For more information about other user setup settings, see Lesson 18.

To change new message options, follow these steps:

1. Open the File menu and choose the Tools command. From the cascading menu that appears, choose User Preferences. You'll see the cc:Mail Preferences dialog box.

2. On the left side, click the Prepare icon. The dialog box changes to look like the one in Figure 8.2.

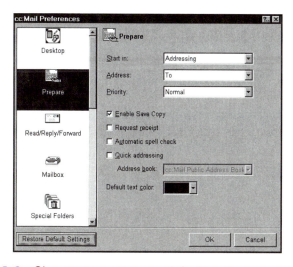

FIGURE 8.2 Change new message default options.

3. Modify any options and choose OK when you are done (refer to Table 8.1).

SETTING DEFAULT OPTIONS FOR MESSAGES YOU RECEIVE

Just as you can set options for new messages you create, you also can tell cc:Mail how to handle messages you receive. For example, you can set defaults for how forwarded messages appear, how replies appear, and so on. Table 8.2 describes the options you can set for messages you receive.

TABLE 8.2   MESSAGE OPTIONS

OPTION	DESCRIPTION
Read Area	
Add author to Personal Address Book	When this box is checked, cc:Mail automatically adds, to your Personal Address Book, the author of any message you read.
Reply Area	
Include reply separator	When this box is checked, your message replies display the original message near the bottom of the Message pane, separated from your reply area by a line.
Forward Area	
Include forward separator	When you check this box, your forwarded message displays the original message near the bottom of the Message pane, separated from your reply area by a line.
Include forwarding history	When you check this box, your forwarded message displays information from the header of the original message as well as the text.

To change options for messages your receive, follow these steps:

1. Open the File menu and choose the Tools command. From the cascading menu that appears, choose User Preferences. You'll see the cc:Mail Preferences dialog box.

2. On the left side, click the Read/Reply/Forward icon. The dialog box changes to look like the one in Figure 8.3.

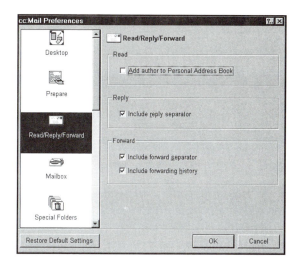

FIGURE 8.3   Change options for messages you receive.

3. Modify any options and choose OK when you are done (refer to Table 8.2).

In this lesson, you learned to set special handling options, to set defaults for new messages you create, and to set defaults for messages you receive. In the next lesson, you'll learn to organize your incoming and outgoing mail.

9 ORGANIZING MAIL

In this lesson, you'll learn to manage your messages using techniques that sort and find messages; you'll also learn to use the Sent Mail folder and the Trash container.

UNDERSTANDING MAIL ORGANIZATION

In previous lessons, you learned to organize your mail by moving it to various containers in the Folder pane, storing it, and saving it. By placing messages in folders, you organize them so you can quickly and easily find specific messages when you need them.

Using containers, such as Drafts and Sent Mail, makes it easy to view stored messages from the Mailbox window as well as use any of the stored mail. Containers help you organize and manage your stored messages, making the following tasks easier to perform:

- Reading and replying to messages about related topics

- Forwarding or re-sending related messages

- Printing the messages pertaining to a specific topic

- Storing messages for future reference by making them easy to find

- Moving messages to other containers and folders by dragging them to the new location, thus keeping your work organized

- Copy messages to other containers for organizational purposes

- Deleting messages that are no longer relevant

- Searching for specific messages

- Attaching, importing, or exporting associated files to your mail message

For More Information See Lesson 5 for information about forwarding, printing, deleting, and saving a message to a folder.

You've already learned to store and organize mail in the following ways:

- **Folders** You can store messages in various folders on the network drive, depending on the drive capacity and the number of messages you want to store (Lesson 5). Folders, in cc:Mail, do not represent directories on your hard disk as they do in Windows 95. Instead, they are an internal way of storing documents in the cc:Mail database files.

Naming Folders Name the folders you create to reflect a project, customer, service, report, or other easily identifiable label; then store only the messages relating to that topic in the folders. That way, you can use folders for a short-term storage and create your own personal filing system.

- **Draft container** You can temporarily store messages until you're ready to send or cancel them (see Lesson 7).

- **Saving messages as files** You can save a message to a file on your hard drive, so that you can use it in another program (see Lesson 7). You can open a saved text file in cc:Mail and then treat it as any other mail message. But remember, the address and header information is not saved with the text file.

The Sent Mail, Trash, and Local Archives are additional containers in the Folder pane of the Mailbox window that will help you organize your mail. The Local Archives container is covered in Lesson 10, but the Sent Mail and Trash containers are covered in this lesson.

SORTING MESSAGES

You will find, at times, that the volume of mail you receive is overwhelming. Although you'd like to move the messages into containers to organize them, you're not sure where to begin. Sometimes, just sorting the mail will help. You can sort your mail in the cc:Mail mailbox window. By default, cc:Mail sorts your messages by author (see Figure. 9.1).

Alphabetical?   At first glance, messages may not appear to be in alphabetical order—at least the way you might alphabetize. That's because cc:Mail doesn't really know a first name from a last name, and if your message senders are using friendly names, cc:Mail sorts by friendly name. Consider Figure 9.1. Elaine comes before Ellen, alphabetically.

To sort messages, you can·use the gray bar at the top of the Message List pane. Click in a portion of the gray bar to sort the messages according to the style you want. For example, to sort by the date the message was received, click Received (see Figure 9.2).

You may notice a small arrow in the gray bar next to one of the titles. That arrow helps you identify the current sort order. If the arrow is pointing up, the items in the list are being sorted from earliest to latest. If the arrow is pointing down, the items in the list are being sorted in reverse order—from latest to earliest.

For example, to sort messages by date from newest to oldest (latest to earliest), click Received so that the arrow points down.

Click any of
these to sort.

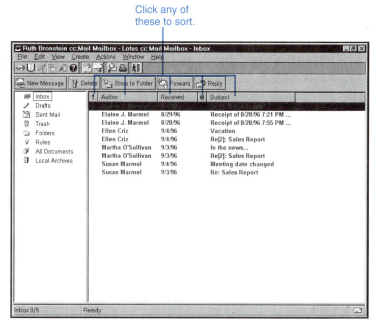

FIGURE 9.1 You can sort messages in the Mailbox window.

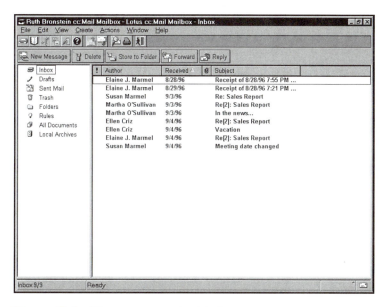

FIGURE 9.2 The messages in this figure are sorted by the date they were received.

WORKING WITH THE TRASH CONTAINER

Now that you've got your messages sorted, let's do something with them. As you read them, you may reply, but you do need to decide what to do with the original messages. You've already learned, in Lesson 5, that you can move the message to a folder in the Folders container.

And, you already know you can delete any message in the Mailbox window by selecting it and pressing the Delete key (also Lesson 5). You can also delete a message by dragging it to the Trash container. Regardless of the method you choose, when you delete a message, cc:Mail displays a confirmation dialog box, asking if you want to move the message.

As you'll see later in this lesson, you can set your options so that all messages in the Trash container remain there for a day, a week, or a month, whatever period of time you need to be sure that you will no longer need them. Thus, the Trash container is an extra storage area for your messages.

USING THE TRASH CONTAINER

You can view the contents of the Trash container by clicking it in the Folder pane (see Figure 9.3)

Even though a message is in the Trash container, you can open, edit, or print the message; if the message you deleted was a message you created, you can even open the message and send it from the Trash container. Or, if you change your mind about deleting a message, you can drag the message from the Trash to any other container or folder.

Once you are certain you no longer need messages in the Trash container, you can personally empty the trash, or you can wait until the time designated in your User Preferences options and let cc:Mail automatically empty the trash. To personally empty the Trash container, click the Empty Trash button on the Action bar. cc:Mail does not wait to confirm this deletion. As the trash is being deleted, however, a dialog box appears showing the progress of the deletion. This dialog box contains a Cancel button you can click to cancel the deletion, but you'll have to act quickly; the dialog box flashes only momentarily.

Clicking this icon opens the Trash container.

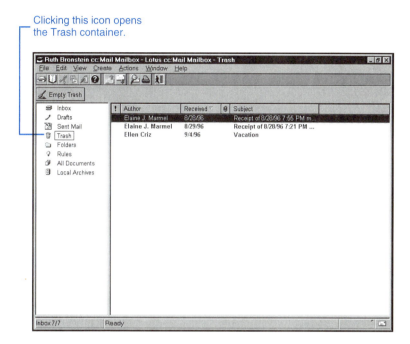

FIGURE 9.3 Messages in the Trash Container.

SETTING TRASH OPTIONS

By default, the messages you move to the Trash container remain there until you delete them or until the time designated for their removal; if you close cc:Mail and then reopen the program, the messages will still be in the Trash container. You can, however, change the options for emptying trash.

To set Trash Options, follow these steps:

1. Open the File menu, and choose the Tools command. From the cascading menu that appears, choose User Preferences . cc:Mail displays the Preferences dialog box.

2. Select the Special Folders icon in the column on the left side of the dialog box to display the options available for the Trash container (see Figure 9.4).

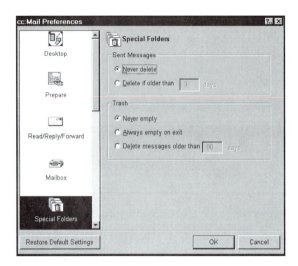

Figure 9.4   Use this dialog box to set preferences for the Trash container.

3. In the Trash area of the dialog box, choose from the following options:

- **Never empty**   When you select this option, all messages remain in the Trash container until you empty the trash. But you should be sure to periodically empty the trash because those messages take up disk space.

- **Always empty on exit**   When you select this option, cc:Mail permanently deletes all messages in the Trash container each time you exit cc:mail.

- **Delete messages older than 90 days**   When you select this option, you can select how many days you want to keep mail in the Trash container before cc:Mail empties the trash for you.

4. Choose OK when you're done to close the dialog box.

WORKING WITH THE SENT MAIL CONTAINER

Up until now, we've focused on organizing the mail you receive. Now let's take a look at what you can do with mail you send.

USING THE SENT MAIL CONTAINER

The Sent Mail container stores copies of the messages you have sent. You can display a message by clicking the Sent Mail container in the Folders pane (see Figure 9.5). You can work with the messages in the Sent Mail container just as you would any message—you can open, edit, print, or even resend a message.

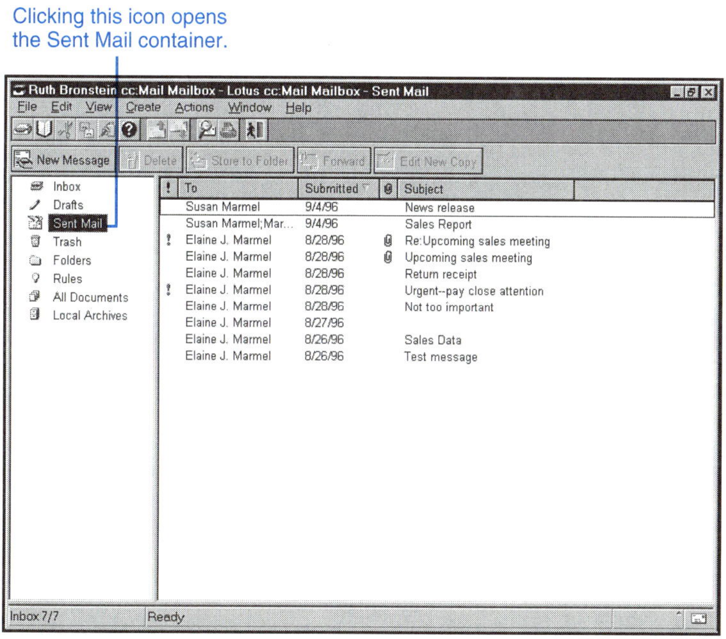

Clicking this icon opens
the Sent Mail container.

FIGURE 9.5   The Sent Mail container, by default, automatically stores copies of the messages you send.

SETTING OPTIONS FOR SENT MAIL

You can set options for Sent Mail that tell cc:Mail whether to automatically delete messages you create; if you choose to automatically delete messages, you also can specify when they should be deleted from the Sent Mail container.

TIP   **Disable Sent Mail**   You can choose to disable cc:Mail's default setting of saving copies of the messages you create. In the cc:Mail Preferences dialog box, choose the Prepare icon. Then, remove the check from the Enable Save Copy check box.

To set Sent Mail options, follow these steps:

1. Open the File menu, and choose the Tools command. From the cascading menu that appears, choose User Preferences. cc:Mail displays the Preferences dialog box.

2. Select the Special Folders icon in the column on the left side of the dialog box. You'll see the same dialog box displayed in Figure 9.4.

3. In the Sent Messages area, choose one of the following options:

  • **Never delete**   This is the default option; however, if you choose to use this setting, you'll need to periodically open the Sent Mail container and delete messages.

  • **Delete messages older than 90 days**   Select this option and fill in the number of days you want to keep messages.

No Disk Space?   If you choose **Never Delete** Messages and do not periodically delete the stored messages, you'll soon have no available disk space on your network drive.

4. Choose OK to close the dialog box or Cancel if you didn't make any changes.

SEARCHING THROUGH THE MAILBOX FOR MESSAGES

As you've seen, you'll store messages in various containers as you work in cc:Mail. After a while, you'll find it difficult to locate specific messages, and sorting messages just won't be sufficient. Using cc:Mail's Search bar, you can locate messages using a variety of different criteria, including the message's subject, author, date, or even the contents of the message.

When you search, you first select a container to search. Then, you tell cc:Mail to match conditions in its search for a message; for example, you might search for any messages whose author is Marmel. Or, you may want to use multiple conditions—say you want to search for all messages whose author is Marmel and whose message text contained the word "sales."

Want to Search through the Entire Mailbox?   If you want cc:Mail to search through all the messages in your mailbox, regardless of container, choose to search the All Documents container.

To search the subject, author, and message text for a word or phrase, follow these steps:

1. In the Mailbox window, click the Search SmartIcon, press Ctrl+Q or open the View menu and choose Search Bar. The Search bar appears just above the Action bar (see Figure 9.6).

2. Select the container you want to search.

3. Type the word or phrase in the text box on the Search bar and press Enter. In the Message List pane, cc:Mail displays only the messages that contain the word or phrase you provided.

Search bar

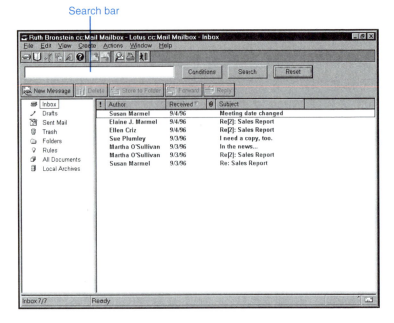

Figure 9.6 Use the Search bar to search for messages.

Finished Searching? When you want to redisplay all messages, click the Reset button on the Search bar. You can remove the search bar by clicking the Search SmartIcon again , or by selecting Search Bar from the View menu again.

To search for messages based on some criteria other than message text, follow these steps:

1. Clear any previous searches by clicking the Reset button on the Search bar.

2. Select the container you want to search.

3. Click the Conditions button in the Search bar to display the Search Conditions dialog box.

4. Open the list box on the left and choose a search criterion, such as **Subject** or **Author**.

5. Open the list box on the right and choose a condition, such as **Contains**.

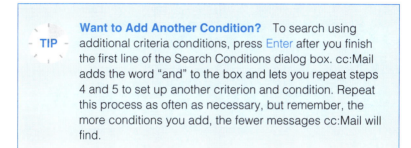

Want to Add Another Condition?   To search using additional criteria conditions, press Enter after you finish the first line of the Search Conditions dialog box. cc:Mail adds the word "and" to the box and lets you repeat steps 4 and 5 to set up another criterion and condition. Repeat this process as often as necessary, but remember, the more conditions you add, the fewer messages cc:Mail will find.

6. When the conditions are set (see Figure 9.7), choose OK to establish the criteria and close the dialog box.

FIGURE 9.7   Narrow cc:Mail's search using the Search Conditions dialog box.

7. Click the Search button in the Search bar to tell cc:Mail to start the search.

Figure 9.8 shows the Inbox before searching, and Figure 9.9 shows a sample search of the Inbox that looked for messages with **Sales** in the subject line and whose author is **Marmel**.

Closing the Search bar   To hide the Search bar, open the View menu, choose Search Bar, remove the check that appears on the menu, and close the Search bar.

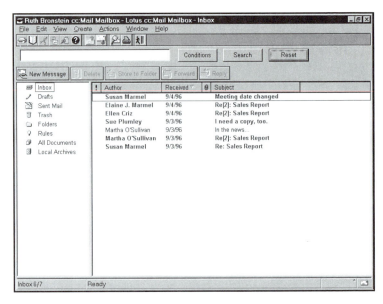

FIGURE 9.8   The Inbox before searching.

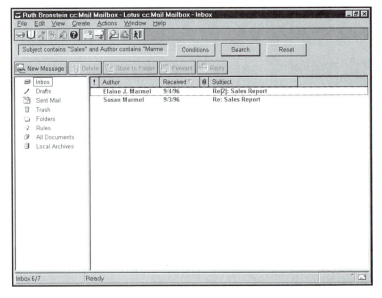

FIGURE 9.9   The Inbox after searching.

In this lesson, you learned to sort messages you receive so that you can more easily organize them by moving them into folders. You also learned how to use the Trash container and the Sent Mail container to manage your mail. Lastly you learned how to search for specific messages. In the next lesson, you'll learn to archive messages.

LESSON 10 ARCHIVING MESSAGES

In this lesson, you'll learn to create an archive, add messages to the archive and delete an archive.

UNDERSTANDING ARCHIVING

The Local Archives container is another place for you to save your e-mail messages. Within the Local Archives container, you can create as many archives as you want and use them to organize and store your mail. Each archive is a file to itself, with a name and a location that you specify on your hard drive, instead of on the server or other network drive.

Archive An archive is a folder found in the Local Archives container in which you can store your e-mail messages for future reference. Think of an archive as a long-term storage container.

Archived messages can be opened only in cc:Mail. You can add a message to your archives at any time; however, you cannot delete or move an individual message from an archive. You can delete or move an entire archive, if you want.

CREATING AN ARCHIVE

You can create as many archives on your hard disk as you want, depending on the amount of disk space you have available. As you add messages to the archive, the archive file becomes larger and larger.

To create an archive, follow these steps:

1. Open the Mailbox window.

2. Open the Create menu and choose the Local Archive command. The Create/Import Archive dialog box appears (see Figure 10.1).

FIGURE 10.1   Use this dialog box to create an archive file.

3. From the Save In list box, choose a drive and folder in which to save your archive, then enter a name for the file in the File Name text box. cc:Mail automatically adds the extension .CCA to the file name.

4. Choose Save. cc:Mail adds the archive folder to the Local Archives container (see Figure 10.2).

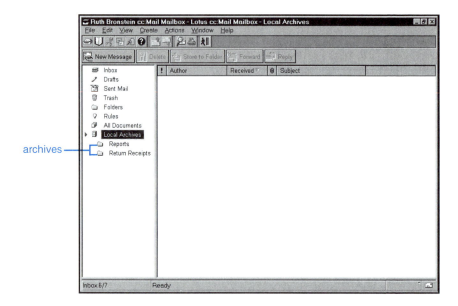

FIGURE 10.2   In this figure, two archives have been added to the Local Archives container.

ADDING MESSAGES TO AN ARCHIVE

You add messages to an archive just as you would add a message to any other folder or container; drag the message to the new container or use the Store to Folder command button.

After you add a message to the archive, you can view, open, read, print, reply to, and otherwise work with the message. You cannot, however, delete the message from the archive.

TIP   **Viewing an Archive**   You can view the contents of an archive by clicking its icon in the Folder pane of the Mailbox.

The easiest way to add a message to an archive is to drag it from its current pane to the archive folder. To use the Store to Folder command button to add a message to an archive, follow these steps:

1. In the Folders pane of the Mailbox window, highlight the Inbox, Drafts, Sent Mail, or other container that contains the message you want to archive.

2. In the Message List pane, highlight the message.

3. Click the Store to Folder button in the Action bar or open the Actions menu and choose the Store to Folder command. The Store Message dialog box appears (see Figure 10.3).

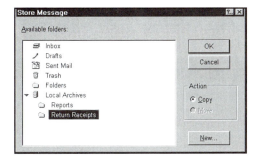

FIGURE 10.3   You can use this dialog box to move or copy a message to an archive folder.

4. In the Available Folders area, highlight the name of the archive to which you want to add the message.

 Can't See the Folder?   If you can't see the archive folder to which you want to add the message, double-click the Local Archives icon in the Folder pane.

5. Choose Copy or Move, depending upon whether you want to archive a copy or the original message.

6. Choose OK. cc:Mail displays a confirmation message and then copies or moves the message to the appropriate archive.

Deleting an Archive

You cannot delete one message within an archive; if you highlight a message in an archive, you'll notice that the Delete button on the Action bar appears dimmed, indicating that it isn't available (see Figure. 10.4)

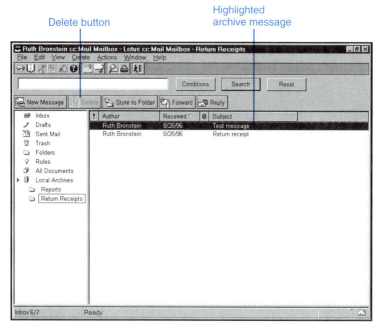

Figure 10.4   You cannot delete an archived message; when you highlight a message in an archive folder, the Delete button on the Action bar dims.

However, you can delete an archive and simultaneously delete all the messages in the archive; when you highlight the archive folder in the Folder pane, you'll notice that the Delete button on Action bar is available. You might want to delete an archive when you no longer need any of the messages it contains.

Deleting isn't really deleting When you delete an archive file, cc:Mail doesn't actually delete the information; the archive folder simply "disappears" from the Folder pane. If you want to retrieve the deleted archive, go through the steps of creating, but don't assign a new file name—instead choose the name of the deleted archive. (You will learn how to permanently delete an archive in a moment).

To delete an archive, follow these steps:

1. Expand the Archives container and double-click the one you want to delete.

2. Press the Delete key. cc:Mail displays a confirmation dialog box asking if you want to delete the archive from the Mailbox.

3. Choose OK to delete the archive.

Save Some Archived Messages You can choose to save some messages in an archive that you're deleting by saving those messages to a new archive; then delete the old archive.

Really Deleting To permanently delete an archive folder, you must find the folder (using, for example, the Windows 95 Explorer) and delete it. Since Local Archive file names end in .CCA, you can search for all files ending in .CCA.

In this lesson, you learn to create an archive, add messages to the archive, and delete an archive. In the next lesson, you learn to work with attached files.

LESSON 11

INCLUDING FILES IN MESSAGES

In this lesson, you'll learn to attach a file to a message, to view an attached file, to save an attached file, and to delete an attachment.

WORKING WITH ATTACHMENTS

You already know that you can send e-mail messages using cc:Mail. In addition to e-mail, you can also send files from other programs with which you work. One way to send a file is to attach it to a message.

 Attachment Any file you send with a message, including an executable (program) file, a compressed file, clipboard contents, forms, text, graphics, faxes, and sound.

ATTACHING A FILE

When you attach a file to a cc:Mail message, the recipient can view the file, and perhaps even edit it, in the file's original application. You can attach any type of file (for example, 1-2-3, Excel, Word, or Word Pro files); attached files retain their formatting.

 TIP **Multiple Attachments** You can attach up to 20 files to a message, depending upon the files' formatting and size.

To attach a file to a message, follow these steps:

1. In the Mailbox window, click the New Message button on the Action bar. cc:Mail displays the New Message window. Create your message by filling in the address, subject line, and message text.

2. Click the Attach SmartIcon. The Attach File dialog box appears (see Figure 11.1).

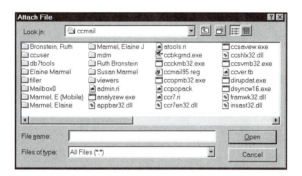

FIGURE 11.1   Use this dialog box to choose one or more files to add as attachments.

3. In the Look in folder, select the path to the file you want to attach.

4. From the list of files, select the file you want to attach.

TIP   **Adding More Than One Attachment**   If you want to add several attachments all from the same folder, use Window 95 file selection techniques. To select a group of adjacent files, click the first file you want to attach, hold down the Shift key, then click the last file you want to attach. To highlight non-adjacent files, click the first file you want to attach, hold down the Ctrl key and click the next file you want to attach and so.

5. Click the Open button. cc:Mail adds an icon to the message portion of the New Message window (see Figure 11.2).

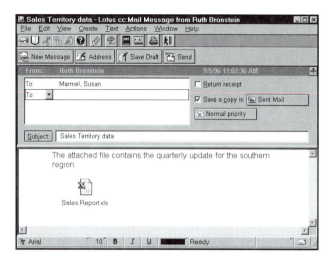

FIGURE 11.2   An icon for the attached file appears in the message text portion of the New Message window. The icon of the attached file indicates the type of document attached to the message; this attachment is an Excel file.

If you want to send multiple attachments but they aren't all located in the same folder, simply repeat these steps. You also can attach graphics, sound, spreadsheets, and other files to a message using the same steps as previously described. The Attach Files dialog box lists, by default, all file types in any selected folder or directory so you can choose the type of file—DOC, WAV, EXE, PCX, LOG, and so on—that you want.

Send the message by pressing Ctrl+S or clicking the Send button on the Action bar. cc:Mail sends the message and returns to the Mailbox window.

VIEWING AN ATTACHED FILE

When you receive a file attached to an e-mail message in cc:Mail, you can view it in cc:Mail's file viewer. The file viewer displays the text so that you can read or view it but you cannot edit the file.

File Viewer   The file viewer is a mini-application that is generally installed with cc:Mail. The file viewer lets you view the contents of an attached file within the message window. If you do not have a file viewer, see your system administrator about reinstalling cc:Mail.

To view an attachment, follow these steps:

1. Open the message containing the attachment (see Figure 11.3).

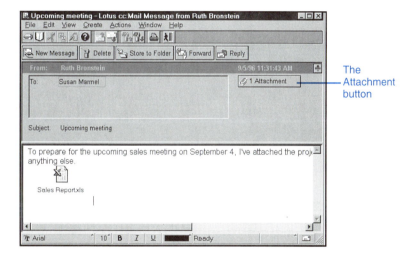

FIGURE 11.3   When a message you receive contains an attachment, you see the attachment icon in the window and you also see an Attachment button.

2. In the Message window, click the Attachment button next to the address area. cc:Mail displays the Attachments window.

3. Highlight the attachment you want to see and click the View button. cc:Mail displays the file in the file viewer (see Figure 11.4).

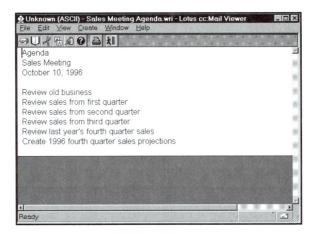

FIGURE 11.4   You can read the attachment text but you cannot edit it in any way.

4. When you're done viewing, return to the message by clicking the Close (X) button in the upper right corner of the viewer's window.

5. Close the Attachments dialog box by clicking the Close (X) button.

6. Reply to the message while it is still open or close the message.

LAUNCHING AN APPLICATION TO WORK WITH AN ATTACHED FILE

If your hard disk contains a copy of the application that created the attached file, you can do more than view the attachment, you can edit it by launching the application. Launching the application opens it within cc:Mail. You work in the launched application just as you would normally; then save the file and exit like always.

Launch Launching is the term used for opening or starting an application from within another application.

To launch an application within cc:Mail, follow these steps:

1. Open the message you received that contains the attachment you want to open within its application.

2. Click the Attachments button in the Message window to display the Attachments dialog box. Highlight the attachment you want to open and click the Launch button. cc:Mail minimizes, and the application in which the attachment was created opens (see Figure 11.5).

 Alert! If cc:Mail doesn't recognize the file extension—such as DOC, WK4, WRI, and so on—it displays the Alert dialog box. Choose Associate and then select the application you want that extension associated with in the future. Exit the dialog box.

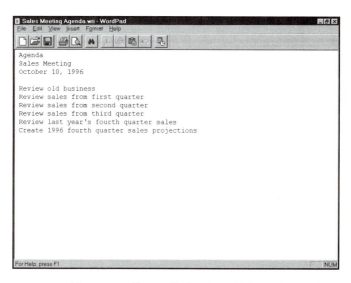

FIGURE 11.5 You can edit, spell check, add formulas or formatting, and otherwise modify the document in its original application.

3. When you're finished, choose File, Save; then choose File, Exit. The application closes and cc:Mail maximizes to fill the screen, displaying the Attachments dialog box.

4. Click the Close (X) button to return to the message.

SAVING THE ATTACHMENT

You can save an attachment so you can open the file later within the original application.

To save an attachment, follow these steps:

1. Open the message you received that contains the attachment you want to save.

2. Click the Attachments button in the Message window to display the Attachments dialog box.

3. Highlight the attachment you want to save and click the Save button. The Save As dialog box appears (see Figure 11.6).

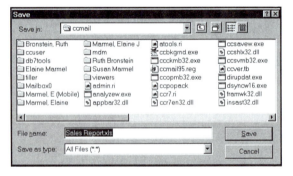

FIGURE 11.6   Save an attachment to your hard drive.

4. From the Save In box, select a location for the file.

5. In the File name text box, provide a name for the new file you're saving.

6. Click the Save button. cc:Mail saves the file and redisplays the Attachments dialog box.

7. Click the Close (X) button to return to the Message window.

DELETING AN ATTACHMENT

If you attach a file to a message, you can delete it before you send the message. However, you cannot delete an attachment to a message someone else has sent you. To delete an attachment in a message you receive, you should delete the entire message just as you would delete any other message.

To delete an attachment in a message you are creating, select the attachment in the message text pane and press the Delete key.

EMBEDDING AND LINKING FILES

Because cc:Mail 7 is OLE 2.0 compatible, you can use two other techniques to send files you have already created: you can embed them or link them. Whether you embed or link a file, you make a copy of the original file that the recipient can actually edit—even if he doesn't own a copy of the application that created the file.

OLE 2.0 Compatible   OLE stands for Object Linking and Embedding. When a program uses version 2.0 of OLE, the program is capable of storing actual data and maintaining links to files that were created in other OLE 2.0-compatible programs. cc:Mail 7 is OLE compatible.

EMBEDDING FILES

When you embed a file, any updates made by the recipient affect only the embedded file; your original file remains unchanged. To embed an existing file in a new message that you are creating, follow these steps:

1. Place the insertion point in the Message Text pane of the message.

2. Open the Create menu and choose the Object command. You'll see the Insert Object dialog box.

3. Click the Create from File option button and the view of the dialog box changes (see Figure 11.7).

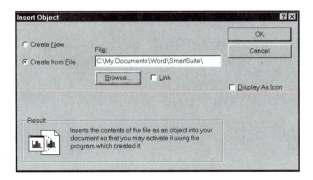

FIGURE 11.7   From this dialog box, locate the file you intend to embed in the message.

4. In the File text box, type the location of the file you want to embed; or, use the Browse button to find the file.

5. Click OK. You'll see an icon in the Message Text pane representing the file you embedded (see Figure 11.8).

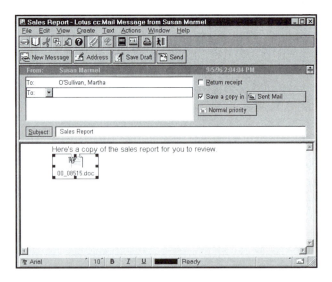

FIGURE 11.8   An embedded file.

LINKING FILES

When you link a file, any updates made by the person who receives the file are also made to your original copy of the file.

To link a file, you follow the steps listed for embedding a file with one exception. Before you click OK in the Insert Object dialog box, place a check in the Link check box that appears next to the Browse button. The icon for the linked file that appears in the Message Text pane will look just like the icon for an embedded file.

In this lesson, you learned to attach a file to a message, to view an attached file, to launch an application to work with an attached file, to delete an attachment, to embed a file, and to link a file. In the next lesson, you will learn to import and export files from other applications.

LESSON 12

IMPORTING AND EXPORTING TEXT FILES

In this lesson, you'll learn to import text to cc:Mail from other applications, as well as to export text from cc:Mail to other applications.

IMPORTING FILES

When you import text, you "paste" the text into the message area of an open Message window. You can only import straight text files; files containing formatting, graphics, and so on will not allow for importing. File types other than text files should be attached rather than imported to a message.

> **TIP**   **Attach a File**   See Lesson 11 for more information about attaching files to cc:Mail messages.

You can import text files from your hard drive or from the network drive. Once you import text to a message, it becomes part of the message just like the text you type into a message.

>
>
> **Text File**   Before you can import a text file, the file must have been saved in the original application as a Text Only file. In most applications—such as Microsoft Word, Lotus Word Pro, Excel, and so on—you choose File, Save As and in the Save As dialog box, change the file type to Text Only, Text Only with line Breaks, or ASCII text.

To import a text file into the Message Text pane of a message you are creating, follow these steps:

1. In the Message window, position the insertion point within the Message Text pane.

2. Choose File, Import. The Import dialog box appears (see Figure 12.1).

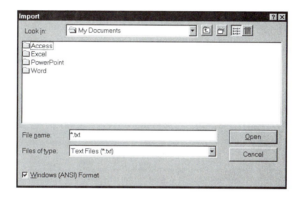

FIGURE 12.1   Select the file you want to import.

3. In the Look in list box, choose the folder containing the file you want to import.

4. Select the file you want to import.

Windows (ANSI) Format   In most cases, you'll want to check the Windows (ANSI) Format check box (which is the default). Remove the check mark in the check box only if you're importing a text file that uses extended characters from another character set, such as with a line draw program.

5. Click the Open button. The file is imported to the message text. In figure 12.2, you see a straight text document imported to a cc:Mail message.

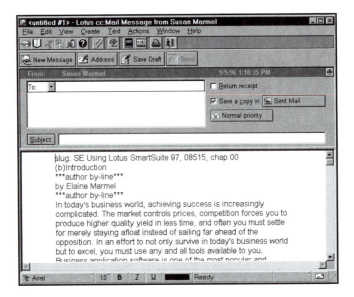

FIGURE 12.2   No formatting is retained in the imported text document.

Garbage on Your Screen?   If, when you import text, you get garbage on your screen—strange characters, one or two repeated characters, at (@) signs, pound (#) signs, and so on—you've tried to import a file that is not a text file. Delete the text and try again, but this time, first save the file in its original application as a TXT file.

TIP

Tabs in Imported Text   When you import tabbed text into the message, cc:Mail's tab stops override the text's settings and cannot be changed. Modify tab stops in the cc:Mail message before importing the text.

TIP

Copy and Paste   You can always *import* a few lines of text from a file to a cc:Mail message by opening the application the file was created in, selecting and copying the lines of text, switching to the open cc:Mail message, and pasting the text in the message.

EXPORTING TEXT

You can select the text in any message and export it to a file. Exporting the text in a message saves only that text, as opposed to saving a message, which saves the text and the addressing information, subject, and so on.

When you export text, you save the text as a text-only file. You can then open the file in various applications as a text file.

To export text from a message, follow these steps:

1. Open the message containing the text you want to export and position the insertion point in the Message Text pane.

TIP

Export Only Part Of The Text   By default, cc:Mail exports all of the text in the Message Text pane. If you want to export only part of the text in the Message Text pane, select only that text.

2. Open the File menu and choose Export. The Export dialog box appears (see Figure 12.3).

3. In the Save in list box, choose a location for the text file.

4. In the File Name text box, enter a name for the text file.

5. Click Save. cc:Mail saves the message text as a text file.

FIGURE 12.3   Use this dialog box to export message text to a text only file.

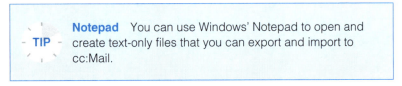

Notepad   You can use Windows' Notepad to open and create text-only files that you can export and import to cc:Mail.

In this lesson, you learned to import and export files in cc:Mail. In the next lesson, you'll learn to use bulletin boards.

Using a Bulletin Board

In this lesson, you'll learn about bulletin boards, how to read messages from a bulletin board and how to reply to bulletin board messages.

Understanding a Bulletin Board

In cc:Mail, a bulletin board is an electronic version of the traditional cork bulletin boards you're familiar with at your home or office. You use cc:Mail bulletin boards to post and read public messages. You create and send messages to the bulletin board the same way you create and send e-mail messages, but bulletin board messages typically reach a much wider audience. Everyone who has access to the bulletin board can read and respond to your bulletin board messages.

Post a Message   When you're sending a message to a bulletin board, it's called "posting" because you're actually displaying your message for all to see.

The cc:Mail administrator creates various bulletin board topics that you can view from the Bulletin Board window. To see the topics available in the Bulletin Board window, open the Window menu and choose Bulletin Boards. Figure 13.1 shows five bulletin boards listed in alphabetical order. The Training bulletin board is highlighted so that you can see the messages it contains. The Bulletin Board window works like the Mailbox window—when you highlight a topic in the folders pane, you see the contents of the topic on the right side of the window.

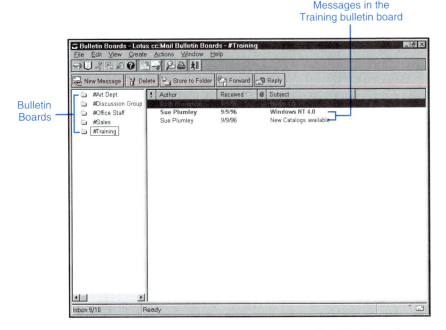

Messages in the
Training bulletin board

Bulletin
Boards

FIGURE 13.1   View and read messages in the Bulletin Board.

The folders in the Bulletin Boards window are organized by topics, and each topic contains related messages you can open, print, respond to, and so on. You cannot, however, delete a bulletin board message unless it is one you have posted yourself. All bulletin board messages are stored on the server.

Pound (#) Sign   Each bulletin board folder is preceded by a pound sign so you can quickly identify it as a bulletin board.

READING A BULLETIN BOARD MESSAGE

You can open a bulletin board message the same way you open messages in the Mailbox window. You highlight the bulletin board, then double-click the message, and cc:Mail displays the

message in its own window (see Figure 13.2). After reading
the message, you can close it, respond to it, forward it, and so on.

Save time reading Bulletin Board messages   You'll
probably find it faster and easier to simply use the Preview Pane when working with Bulletin Board messages.

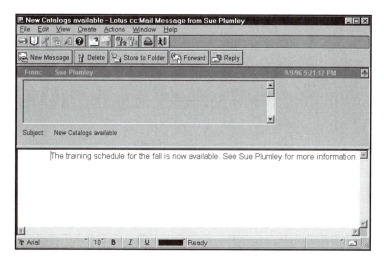

FIGURE 13.2   You can read a bulletin board message in it's own
window.

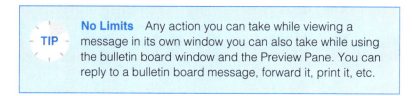

No Limits   Any action you can take while viewing a
message in its own window you can also take while using
the bulletin board window and the Preview Pane. You can
reply to a bulletin board message, forward it, print it, etc.

To read a bulletin board message in the preview pane, follow
these steps:

1. From the Mailbox window, open the Window menu and
choose Bulletin Boards.

2. To display the Preview Pane, open the View menu and choose Show Preview Pane. cc:Mail adds a third pane to the Bulletin Boards window.

3. Click any bulletin board name in the Folders pane to display the messages in that bulletin board. The list of messages for that bulletin board appears in the Contents pane.

4. Highlight the message you want to preview, and its contents appear in the Preview Pane at the bottom of the screen (see Figure 13.3).

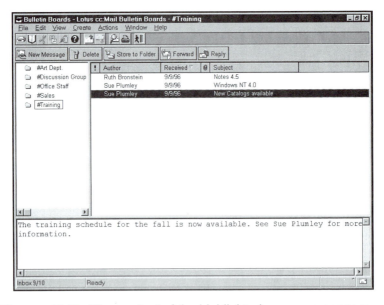

Figure 13.3   The content of the highlighted message appears in the Preview Pane.

PLACING A MESSAGE IN A LOCAL FOLDER

You may want to save a copy of a message you find on a bulletin board. Although you can't drag and drop the message to a local folder, you can copy the message to a folder. Follow these steps:

1. Make sure you are viewing the Bulletin Boards window, then highlight the bulletin board containing the message you want to copy.

2. Highlight the message.

3. Click the Store to Folder button on the Action bar. The Store Message dialog box appears (see Figure 13.4).

4. Highlight the container into which you want to copy the message.

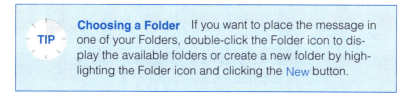

TIP **Choosing a Folder** If you want to place the message in one of your Folders, double-click the Folder icon to display the available folders or create a new folder by highlighting the Folder icon and clicking the New button.

5. Click the Copy button in the Store Message dialog box.

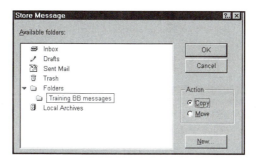

FIGURE 13.4   Use this dialog box to select a local folder in which to store a copy of a bulletin board message.

6. Click OK.

REPLYING TO A BULLETIN BOARD MESSAGE

When you reply to a bulletin board message, your reply will be sent directly to the mailbox of the sender of the original message, not to the bulletin board.

To reply to a bulletin board message, follow these steps:

1. Highlight the message to which you want to reply.

2. Click the Reply button on the Action bar. The Reply dialog box appears (see Figure 13.5).

FIGURE 13.5   When you reply to a bulletin board message, you're replying to the sender, not the bulletin board.

3. Select an option for replying:

- **Reply to sender** While the original message may have been sent to multiple recipients, select this option to reply to only the sender of the message.

- **Reply to sender and all recipients** Select this option to reply to the sender and to all other recipients of the message.

- **Reply to sender with original message** Select this option if you want to reply only to the sender of the message and include, in your reply, the original message text.

- **Reply to sender and all recipients with original message** Select this option to reply to the sender and all other recipients of the message and to include, in your reply, the original message text.

4. In the reply window that appears (see Figure 13.6), type your reply in the bottom pane.

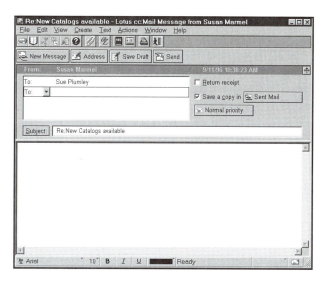

FIGURE 13.6   Use the Reply window to answer a bulletin board message the same way you would reply to e-mail messages.

5. Click the Send Message icon. cc:Mail displays the confirmation dialog box, and then sends your reply.

Reply to Bulletin Board   You may want to reply to the bulletin board instead of to the individual who wrote the message. To do this, you must address the reply to the bulletin board, as described in the following section. You still use the Reply window; however, change the address before sending the message.

CREATING AND SENDING A MESSAGE TO A BULLETIN BOARD

When creating a message for the bulletin board, whether a new message or a reply to a message, you must address the message directly to the bulletin board. You also can send a message to another post office and bulletin board, as long as you enter the bulletin board name exactly as it appears at the other post office.

To create a bulletin board message, follow these steps:

1. In the Bulletin Board window, click the New Message button on the Action bar.

TIP **Reply** After you've read a message to which you want to reply and you've clicked the Reply button, you can use steps 2 through 5 to address your reply.

2. Click the Address button on the Action bar. The Address Book dialog box appears (see Figure 13.8).

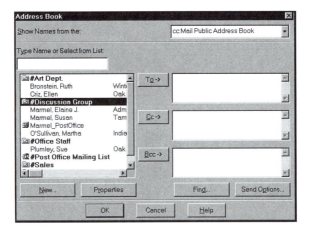

FIGURE 13.8 Bulletin boards appear in the Public Address Book preceded by pound signs (#) for easy identification.

3. Click the bulletin board to which you want to address the message and click the To-> button.

TIP **Multiple Addresses** Notice that you can address a message to multiple bulletin boards or addresses by selecting additional names and choosing the To-> button, the Cc-> button, or the Bcc-> button.

4. Choose OK. The address you chose appears in the Address pane of the message window. You can now enter your message and send it as you normally would. cc:Mail posts the message to the selected bulletin board.

Where's Your Message?   If you don't see your message on the bulletin board right away, be patient. Depending on your network configuration and system setup, it may take some time for the message to post. If you don't see your message on the bulletin board within 24 hours, ask your system administrator what the normal lag time is.

In this lesson, you learned how to use cc:Mail bulletin boards. You learned to read messages from a bulletin board, to reply to bulletin board messages, and to create and send new bulletin board messages. In the next lesson, you'll learn to use cc:Mail forms.

14

USING CC:MAIL FORMS

In this lesson, you'll learn to understand forms, to open forms sent to you in messages, and to attach built-in forms to your own messages.

UNDERSTANDING FORMS

cc:Mail provides several forms that are similar to paper forms (such as Expense reports, Mileage reports, Time Cards, and so on). But they are more efficient in some situations. When several people need to see or add to the same form, for example, it's easier to pass the form back and forth by e-mail than by inter-office messengers or memos.

cc:Mail forms are templates that provide formatting so you can use them over and over again. Following is a list of the cc:Mail form templates:

- Time Card   Contains areas for your name, department, and pay period dates. It also has areas for entering the hours of regular time, overtime, vacation time, and so on. The file name for this form is timecrd.lfm.

- Travel Itinerary/Preference   Includes areas for name and personal information, plus areas for departure method and times, flight numbers, return times and dates, hotel addresses, and so on. The file name for this form is itinry.lfm.

- Computer Hardware/Software Request   Contains areas for your name and personal information, plus areas in which to list your software and hardware needs. The filename for this form is compreq.lfm.

- Travel Expense Reimbursement Request   Contains areas for your name and other information, plus a table in which you enter the dates of travel, air fare, auto rental, lodging, and so on. The file name for this form is expense.lfm.

- Employee Move Notice Includes areas for your new address, e-mail address, phone, pager, and so on and an area for the old address and information. The file name for this form is moving.lfm.

Your mail administrator may design special forms you can use in cc:Mail. You can use forms in various ways. You might send a blank form to others on the network and ask them to fill it out and return it to you. Or, you might need to fill in a form, such as a time card, and attach it to a message to send to others.

TIP **Forms as Attachments** When you send a form with your e-mail messages, you attach the form to the message. For more information about attaching a file to a message, see Lesson 11.

RECEIVING AND FILLING IN A FORM

When you receive a form with a message, typically it will be an attachment that you can open and fill in. To work with a form you received with a message, follow these steps:

1. Open the message. You'll see the form attachment in the Attachments pane of the Message window (see Figure 14.1).

TIP **Viewing and Saving Form Attachments** You can save a form attachment, just like any attachment, by clicking the Attachments button, then clicking the Save button, and then assigning a file name and location. You can view a form attachment by clicking the Attachments button and then clicking the View button.

2. Double-click the attachment to launch it. cc:Mail opens the form in the Forms window (see Figure 14.2).

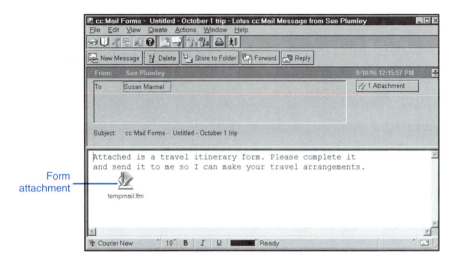

Form attachment

FIGURE 14.1   Form attachments can be saved, viewed, or opened in the Forms window.

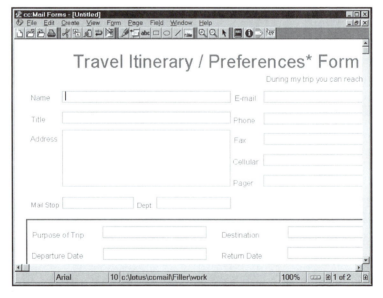

FIGURE 14.2   The form opens as an untitled document.

3. To fill in the form, click the mouse in the area provided and enter the information requested. You can press the Tab key to move from one field to the next field or Shift+Tab to move to the previous field. You can also use the **Enter** key to move from field to field.

Sending a Form

There are several reasons why you may need to send a form:

- Once you've filled in a form, you may need to send it to someone else.

- You may need to start the process by filling in a form and *then* sending it to someone else.

- You might send blank forms by e-mail for others to fill-in.

Whether you send a blank form or one you've filled in, the steps are the same. The only difference is where you start the process. If you received a form from someone else and filled it in using the steps in the last section, you're ready to send. On the other hand, if you need to start the process yourself and send either a blank or filled-in form to someone else, you need to first open the form. To open a form, open the Create menu and choose the Forms command. From the cascading menu that appears (see Figure 14.3), choose the type of form you want to send.

If you intend to send a blank form, proceed to the steps below. If you intend to send the form already filled in, first complete the form using the steps from the last section. Then complete the steps below.

1. Click the Send button you'll find on the form. cc:Mail displays the Send Mail dialog box (see Figure 14.4).

2. Fill in the subject line and any message you want to attach to the form when you send it.

3. Click the Address button. The dialog box changes to include Address Book information (see Figure 14.5)

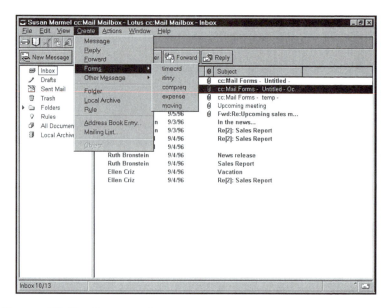

FIGURE 14.3   Choose a form to open.

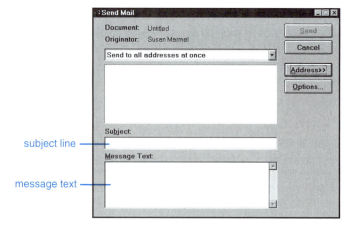

FIGURE 14.4   Use this dialog box to send a form.

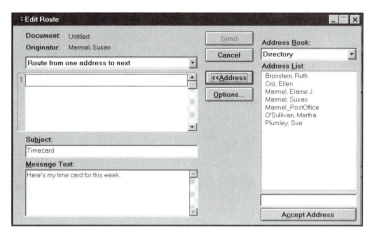

FIGURE 14.5   Address the form using the right side of the dialog box.

4. To address the form, select an address book from the Address Book list box; then highlight an addressee from the Address List. Click the Accept Address button below the Address List.

5. Click the Send button to send the form. cc:Mail displays the Form Send dialog box (see Figure 14.6)

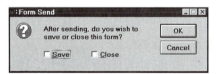

FIGURE 14.6   This dialog box gives you the opportunity to save a copy of your form before you send it.

6. Choose Save to save a copy of the form in the \windows\ temp folder. Choose Close to remove the form from your screen. Then choose OK.

Want Your Own Copy? To save the form in a location and with a name of your choosing, start by opening the File menu and choosing the Save As command. You'll see a dialog box, in which you can navigate to the drive and folder of your choice. Supply a file name and choose OK. Now you're ready to complete Steps 1-6.

In this lesson, you learned about receiving, sending, completing, and saving forms. In the next lesson, you'll learn the cc:Mail "rules," which will help you do things automatically.

GETTING STARTED WITH RULES

In this lesson, you'll learn to view, run, enable, and disable rules.

UNDERSTANDING RULES

Rules are sets of instructions that automate a task. In cc:Mail, a rule executes when a specific event occurs, such as starting or exiting the cc:Mail program or sending a message. You use rules to help you complete your work quickly, effortlessly, and more efficiently. If it's critical that you receive and respond immediately to messages from your boss, for example, a rule.

To show you how a rule works, say your boss e-mails you only when she has something timely and important to tell you. You naturally want to know as soon as any message from your boss arrives. A rule can alert you immediately when you receive mail from your boss. Receiving the mail from that specific person is the event that triggers the automated rule to you.

Rules can be manual or automatic. You might, for example, set a rule to automatically delete all read messages from the Inbox when you exit cc:Mail. On the other hand, you can set a rule so that it runs only when you initiate it, such as a rule that files your incoming messages when you direct it to do so.

VIEWING RULES

cc:Mail doesn't come with any rules, so initially, you won't see anything in the Rules container. However, you view rules by clicking the Rules container in the Folders Pane. The rules appear in the Rules List (see Figure 15.1). Rules consist of several components, as described here:

Description	Describes the rule so that you can recognize it.
When to Run	Determines when the rule is executed.
Enabled	Enables the automatic rule to run, either automatically or manually. A disabled rule cannot run until you enable it.
Last Run	Provides the date on which the rule last ran.
Active From and Active To	Dates defining the period of time the rule is active.
Schedule	A timetable describing when the rule will run; the schedule can be daily, weekly, or monthly.

 Run Running a rule means activating it. An automatic rule runs when an event or scheduled time occurs; a manual rule runs only when you choose to activate it.

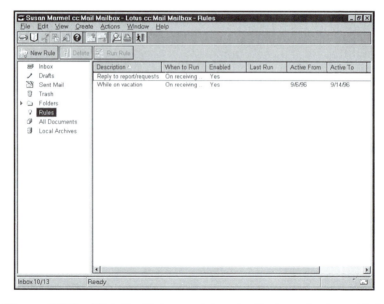

FIGURE 15.1   Click the Rules container to display rules in cc:Mail.

In the list of rules, the description tells you a little about the rule. For example, the first rule states **Reply to report/requests**. If you enlarge the When to Run column, you see that the rule is set to execute when a new message is received.

Column Sizing   To size a column in the Rules List window, position the mouse arrow in the heading bar on the column line. The mouse changes to a two-headed arrow; drag the mouse to widen or shorten the column.

CREATING RULES

To make your life easier, you can create rules that cc:Mail will use to handle special circumstances. Suppose, for example, that you'll be on vacation. Your assistant is going to download your messages for you, but not reply to them. You can create a rule that tells cc:Mail to send a standard reply to messages you receive while on vacation. That way, you can let the sender of the message know that, while it looks like you got the message, you're really on vacation.

You actually create a rule in three stages:

- You provide a name for the rule
- You specify when the rule should run
- You identify what the rule should do when it runs.

We'll create one rule using these three stages in the next three sections. We'll begin by providing a name for the rule.

NAMING A RULE

To name a rule, follow these steps:

1. In the Folders pane, click the Rules container.

2. Click the New Rule button on the Action bar. cc:Mail displays the Rule Viewer window (see Figure 15.2).

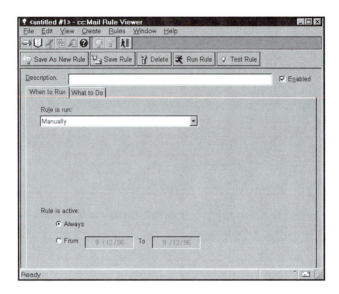

FIGURE 15.2   Use the Rule Viewer window to define rules.

3. In the Description box, type a name for the rule. This name will appear in the Rule list.

SPECIFYING WHEN A RULE SHOULD RUN

You'll use the first tab of the Rule Viewer to determine when cc:Mail runs the rule.

1. Use the Rule is Run list box to select when a rule should run. Your choices are:

- **Manually**   Sets a rule to run only when you select the rule and choose **Rules, Run Rule** in the Rules List window.

- **On exit**   Runs a rule automatically when you exit the program.

- **On mail download**   Runs a rule prior to cc:Mail downloading each message.

- **On receiving message**   Runs a rule automatically when new messages are received in the Inbox.

- **On sending message**   Runs a rule automatically whenever you send a message.

- **On startup**   Runs a rule automatically when you start the cc:Mail program.

- **On the following schedule**   (daily, weekly or monthly)   Runs a rule on the day and time you specify.

Scheduling   When you choose one of the "schedule" options, more information appears in the Rule Viewer to let you create a schedule for cc:Mail to use to run the rule.

2. At the bottom of the dialog box, choose whether the rule should be enabled all the time, or only during a specified period.

Setting the Dates   If you choose **From,** cc:Mail automatically supplies today's date in the boxes. Click any portion of the date and use the Up and Down arrows on the keyboard to increase or decrease the selected number by increments.

DETERMINING THE RULE'S FUNCTION

As explained previously, rules cause cc:Mail to take an action. To create a rule, you not only specify when the action should occur, but you also specify the conditions of the rule's execution.

Condition   Conditions are criteria you set for each rule. A condition describes what the rule is to look for within the message, such as someone's name in the TO area or a specific word in the Subject area of the message.

Specifically, you tell cc:Mail:

- the container on which the rule should operate
- the messages that will be subject to the rule
- the action that cc:Mail will take.

To set conditions and actions for a rule, follow these steps:

1. Click the What to Do tab of the Rule Viewer. cc:Mail displays the What to Do tab (see Figure 15.3)

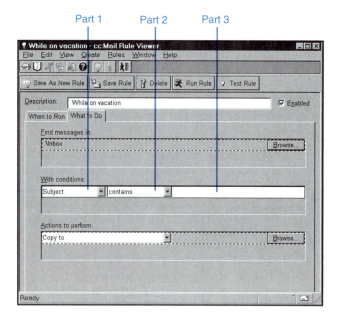

FIGURE 15.3   Use this tab to determine a rule's function.

2. In the Find Messages In area, identify the container cc:Mail should check when running the rule. If the container you want doesn't appear by default, click the Browse button to select it.

3. In the With Conditions area, set the conditions you want cc:Mail to check before running the rule. For ease of explanation, we'll divide the line into three parts, as

shown in the figure. In Part 1, you can tell cc:Mail to check any of the following information about a message:

Age (of message)	Author	bcc
cc	Item contents	Message Type
Priority	Read Status	Receipt returned
Recipients	Send date	Send time
Size	Subject	To

4. Next, select a comparison operator from the Part 2 list box. Your choices depend on the selection you made in the Part 1 list box. For example, if you chose **Subject** in the Part 1 list box, your choices in the Part 2 list box are **Contains**, **Does Not Contain**, **Is**, or **Is Not**. Alternatively, if you chose **Send Date** in the Part 1 list box, your choices in the Part 2 list box are **Is Before**, **Is After**, **Is**, or **Is Not**.

5. In the Part 3 box, supply information for cc:Mail to use when comparing. For example, if you chose **Subject** and **Contains** from the Part 1 and Part 2 list boxes, you might type **Report** in the Part 3 box. If you chose **Send Date** and **Is After** in the Part 1 and Part 2 list boxes, you should supply a date in the Part 3 box.

   The conditions for a vacation response message might be **Send Date**, **Is After**, and **9/9/96** (the first day of your vacation).

6. When you press **Enter** after filling in the Part 3 box, cc:Mail automatically assumes you want to add another condition (see Figure 15.4). If you set multiple conditions for a rule using **and** in the left list box of Figure 15.4, *all* the criteria must be met or cc:Mail won't run the rule. If, alternatively, you choose **or** from the left list box, cc:Mail will run the rule if *either* of the conditions is met.

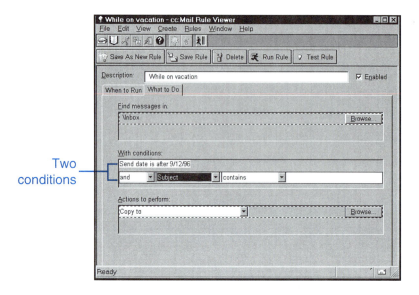

Two conditions

FIGURE 15.4   cc:Mail lets you set multiple conditions for a rule.

7. To set another condition, repeat Steps 3-6. If, for example, you're creating a vacation rule, you'll need to specify the rule's end date. If you don't need to set additional conditions, just skip to the Actions to Perform area.

8. In the Actions to Perform area, choose one of 17 different actions you want cc:Mail to take when the conditions of the rule are met. Use the list box on the left to select the action and then use the box on the right to supply any additional information required by the action. For example, you could choose **Copy To** and then select a folder in which you want the message placed. Or, you could set the rule so that it forwards the messages, like it did in Figure 15.5.

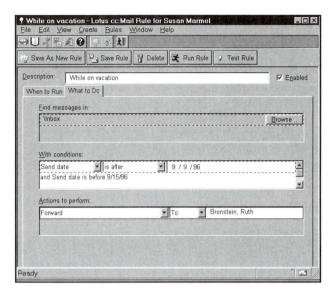

FIGURE 15.5   A sample rule for forwarding messages received while on vacation.

RUNNING RULES MANUALLY OR AUTOMATICALLY

You can run a rule manually or automatically. To run a rule manually, you need to set up the rule so that it is enabled (see Chapter 16 for more information on enabling and disabling rules). Then, on the **When to Run** tab choose any of the following from the **Rule is Run** list box:

- Manually
- On Startup
- On exit
- On a schedule.

You cannot run a rule manually if the run time is any of the following:

- On mail download
- On receiving message
- On sending message.

To run a rule one time, highlight the rule in the Rules List window. The **Run Rule** button on the Action bar is now available; click it.

Alternatively, you can set up a rule to run automatically, whenever its conditions are met. A rule will run automatically if, in the Rule window on the When to Run tab, you select any choice *except* Manually from the Rule is Run list box.

 Change the Run Time of a Rule   To learn how to make changes to a rule, including run time changes, see Chapter 16.

In this lesson, you learned to view, create, and run rules. In the next lesson, you'll learn to modify, delete, and disable rules.

Editing and Managing Rules

In this lesson, you'll learn to modify, delete, and disable rules.

Changing a Rule

After you create a rule, you may decide you need to change something about the way the rule works. You edit the rule in the cc:Mail Rule Viewer window, where you created the rule. On the When to Run tab of that window, you can change the description and run time of the rule, specify whether the rule is enabled, and define when the rule is active. On the What to Do tab, you can modify the rule's function.

Modifying When a Rule Runs

To change when a rule runs follow these steps:

1. In the Rules List window, double-click the rule you want to modify to open the window where you can edit the rule (see Figure 16.1).

>
> **TIP** **Rules List** Display the Rules List window by clicking the Rules container in the Folders pane.

2. To change the name of the rule, select the text in the Description text box and enter a new name or description.

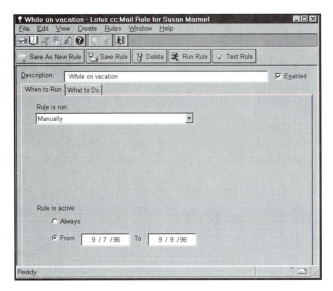

FIGURE 16.1   Use this window to modify rules to suit your needs.

3. To change run time, click the down arrow in the When to Run drop-down list and choose a run time from the drop-down list (see Lesson 15 for a description of the run-time options).

4. Place a check in the Enable check box to automatically run the rule at the appointed time.

Enable a Rule   When a rule is enabled, that means it is available to run. You can select it to run manually, or automatically.

5. If you are finished modifying the rule, save the modifications. Click the Save button to replace the existing rule with your changed rule, or choose Save as New to save a new version of the rule and retain the original version as well.

To modify the rule further, see the next two sections.

MODIFYING WHAT THE RULE WILL DO

Using the What to Do tab, you can modify the container cc:Mail searches while running a rule, the conditions of the rule, and the action a rule takes so that it better suits the way you work. In Figure 16.2, you see the What to Do tab, and I've numbered each part of the condition for easier reference.

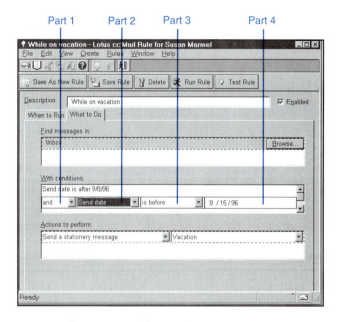

FIGURE 16.2 Change a rule's conditions and actions to suit your working style.

To modify the container cc:Mail searches when attempting to apply the rule, click the Browse button to switch to a different container.

To change a condition, click the line on which the condition appears to activate it. Then, make changes by making selections from the list boxes that appear on the line. See Table 16.1 for a description of your choices.

TABLE 16.1 CONDITION ELEMENTS

ELEMENT	DESCRIPTION
Part 1	Choose And to find messages that match two conditions; choose Or to find messages that find one or the other condition.
Part 2	Select the area of the message you want the rule to search, such as the Subject, Text, Author, Recipient, and so on.
Part 3	Choose from qualifiers such as the Subject line's **contains**, **does not contain**, **is**, or **is not** to further define the rule's conditions.
Part 4	Select specific text to find, such as in the subject line FYI: or RE:, or enter your own text.

Actions describe what the rule does in response to the event. You can modify the actions that have been specified for any rule. Figure 16.3 shows the Actions dialog box.

TIP **Additional Work** Some actions may require additional work in addition to setting up a rule. For example, if you're going to send a message from the draft container, you must create that message and store it in the draft container.

The number of parts you see in the Actions tto Perform area depends on the action you choose. In Figure 16.3, the Actions to Perform area contains two parts, which we've labeled Part 1 and Part 2. Click the drop-down arrow in Part 1, and choose an action—such as **Move to**, **Copy to**, **Delete**, **Mark as Read**, and so on—from the list.

The options for Part 2 depend on the action you choose in Part 1.

For example, if, in Part 1, you choose the **Move to** or **Copy to** action, Part 2 changes to a **Browse** button. You can use this button to open a dialog box and choose the container (archive, folder, and so on) to which you want to move or copy. If, in Part 1, you choose **Print**, Part 2 displays no options at all.

To save changes you make to a rule, choose the **Save** button on the Action bar.

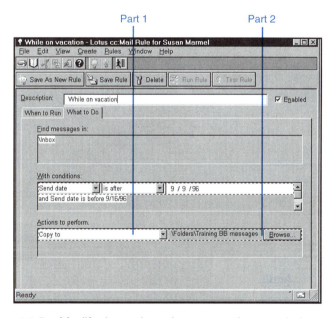

FIGURE 16.3   Modify the actions that occur when a rule is activated.

TIP   **Create a New Rule Using an Existing Rule**   If you find a rule very similar to one you want to create, start by editing the existing rule. Once you have set up the new rule, click the Save As New Rule button on the Action bar. cc:Mail will save the new rule and leave the original rule unchanged.

DELETING RULES

You can delete any rule in the Rules list.

No Undo When you delete a rule, you cannot undo the deletion. If you want to use the rule again, you must recreate it.

To delete a rule, follow these steps:

1. Click the Rules container in the Folders Pane. The Rules list appears.

2. Select the rule(s) you want to delete.

3. Click the Delete button on the Action bar or press the Del key. There is no warning dialog box; cc:Mail simply deletes the rule.

ENABLING AND DISABLING RULES

By default, when you create a rule, cc:Mail enables the rule. You disable a rule when you no longer want it to run. You can easily enable and disable any or all rules any time you want.

Disable a Rule When you disable a rule, the rule still exists (you haven't deleted it), but cc:Mail will not run the rule, even if the conditions exist for the rule to run.

To disable a rule, follow these steps:

1. Double-click the rule in the Rules list.

2. Immediately next to the rule's name, remove the check from the Enabled check box by clicking it once (see Figure 16.4).

Enabled
check box

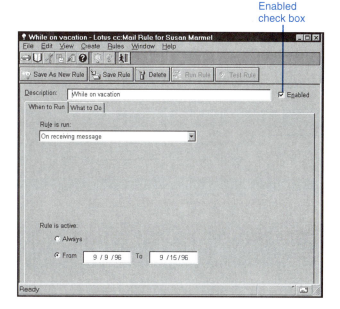

FIGURE 16.4   Placing or removing the check from the Enabled check box determines whether a rule will run.

3. Click the Save Rule button on the Action bar.

In this lesson, you learned to modify, delete, and disable rules. In the next lesson, you'll learn how to use cc:Mail while you're away from the office.

17 ˢᴸᴱˢˢᴼᴺ TRAVELING WITHOUT A COMPUTER

In this lesson, you'll learn to use cc:Mail while you're away from the office and while you're without a computer. You'll learn how to delegate your mailbox and you'll learn how to be a delegate for someone else.

DELEGATING YOUR MAILBOX

Sometimes, you travel away from the office and you don't take a computer. While you're gone, people continue to send you messages. You can *delegate* your mailbox to someone else while you're away. Even though you delegate your mailbox, you can still log in and read, reply to, or forward messages.

 Delegating your mailbox When you delegate your mailbox, you give someone else (called a delegate) access to your Mailbox and the messages it contains. Any rules you set up still apply while your mailbox is delegated.

You can delegate your mailbox only to a user who is running cc:Mail 7 and whose mailbox is also on your post office. To delegate your mailbox to someone else, follow these steps:

1. Open the File menu and choose Delegate Mailbox. cc:Mail displays the Mailbox Delegation dialog box (see Figure 17.1).

2. From the list on the left, select a name and click the Add >> button.

3. Repeat step 2 to assign additional delegates.

4. Choose OK when you finish. cc:Mail displays a message reminding you that only users of cc:Mail 7 can act as delegates. Click OK.

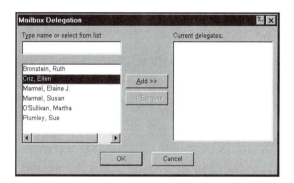

FIGURE 17.1   Use this dialog box to select delegate(s) for your mailbox.

  Going on a trip?   Delegate your mailbox before you leave, because you cannot delegate your mailbox from a remote location.

BEING A DELEGATE

Someone who travels without a computer may delegate their Mailbox to you.

  Being a delegate   When you act as a delegate, you have access to both your mailbox and the mailbox of the person who made you a delegate. Both the traveler and the delegate can read, reply to, and forward messages in the delegated Mailbox.

When someone delegates their Mailbox to you, cc:Mail sends you a message notifying you that you have been assigned as a delegate (see Figure 17.2).

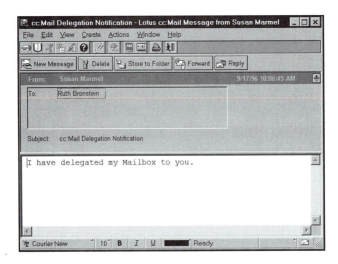

Figure 17.2   You'll receive this message if someone delegates their Mailbox to you.

As a delegate, you can open, reply to, forward, and create messages. You don't need a password to open the delegated Mailbox. Any messages you send as a delegate will contain two names in the From field—the name of the person who delegated the mailbox to you, followed by your name, which will appear in parentheses (see Figure 17.3).

As a delegate you *cannot* do the following while working in the delegated Mailbox:

- Modify the Personal Address Book

- Modify private mailing lists

- Modify User Preferences

- Modify or work with messages in local archives.

The delegate's name

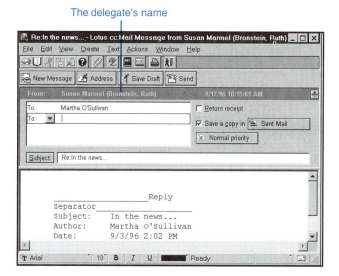

FIGURE 17.3   When you respond to a message as a delegate, your name appears in the From line in (parentheses) after the name of the person who delegated the mailbox.

You can, however, access the delegated Mailbox. To access a Mailbox that has been delegated to you, follow these steps:

1. Open the Window menu and highlight the Other command. On the cascading menu that appears, you'll see the names of the mailboxes that have been delegated to you (see Figure 17.4).

2. Select the Mailbox you want to use. Notice that cc:Mail user's name appears in the title bar at the top of the cc:Mail screen.

3. To return to your own Mailbox, press Alt+F4 or open the File menu and choose the Close command. Your own name reappears in the title bar at the top of the cc:Mail screen.

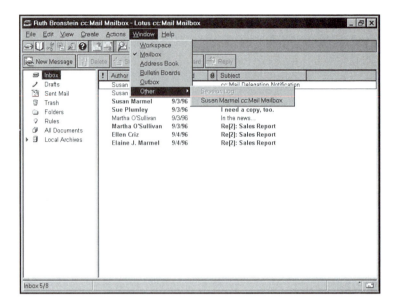

FIGURE 17.4   When someone delegates a Mailbox to you, you'll see their name on your Window menu.

REMOVING A DELEGATE

When you no longer need someone to act as a delegate for you, follow these steps:

1. Open the File menu and choose Delegate Mailbox. cc:Mail displays the Mailbox Delegation dialog box.

2. From the list on the right, select a name and click the Remove button.

3. Repeat step 2 to remove other delegates.

4. Choose OK when you finish. cc:Mail sends the message you see in Figure 17.5 to the former delegate.

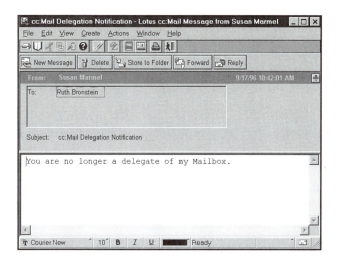

FIGURE 17.5   When someone removes you as a delegate, you see this message.

In this lesson, you learned how to use cc:Mail when you travel without a computer. In the next lesson, you'll learn how to connect to cc:Mail while you're away from your office.

18

CONNECTING TO CC:MAIL WHILE ON THE ROAD

In this lesson, you'll learn how to use cc:Mail away from the office when you travel with a computer.

UNDERSTANDING THE MOBILE CONNECTION

When you travel, you can connect to your company's cc:Mail network and send and receive mail. Typically, you use a notebook computer and a modem, and you're called a *mobile user*.

Mobile User   Someone who uses a telephone line, a computer, and a modem to connect to cc:Mail away from the office rather than on a network.

Modem   A device that allows you to connect computers via telephone lines and to send and receive data.

Methods of Connection   Mobile users can connect to cc:Mail in several ways, including TCP/IP, NetWare SPX, X.25, and PBX, but most mobile users connect using a modem and that's the method we will discuss in this book. Check with your cc:Mail administrator to find out the method of connecting you're supposed to use.

When you work as a mobile user, most of the time you work in cc:Mail without being connected to your post office. You compose messages and then, when you're ready to send them, you connect to the post office. The connection you make may require a long distance telephone call, so this method of working minimizes potential long distance phone charges.

SETTING UP FOR A MOBILE CONNECTION

To create a mobile connection, you need to install cc:Mail on the computer you'll be using while you're away from the office. That computer might be your home computer, or it might be a notebook computer with which you travel. If you need help installing cc:Mail, see your administrator.

 It's not working!   You don't want to find out on-the-road that the modem on the computer you'll be traveling with doesn't work. Your cc:Mail administrator will take care of the modem on the computer containing the post office; you should install, set up, and test the modem on your remote computer before you leave on your trip. Follow the instructions you get from the modem manufacturer or see your cc:Mail administrator for help.

To connect while you're traveling, you need a log-in profile that tells cc:Mail to connect using your modem. Since creating this profile is somewhat lengthy, we'll break up the process a little bit.

SETTING A USER NAME FOR THE MOBILE PROFILE

To get started creating your mobile log-in profile, follow these steps:

1. If you're currently running cc:Mail, exit from the program.

2. Start cc:Mail again, pausing when you see the opening dialog box, where you usually select your profile that connects directly to the post office (see Figure 18.1)

FIGURE 18.1   Set up a mobile profile starting in this dialog box.

3. In the Login/Profile name text box, type your name as you want it to appear in this list box. This name *does not* need to match the format of your user name as specified by your system administrator.

TIP

Mobile Profile Name   You might want to include the word "mobile" in your name to help you distinguish a mobile profile from a network profile.

4. In the Password text box, type the password your system administrator gave you.

5. Choose OK. You'll see a dialog box that explains that you entered the name of a user who has not logged on from this computer previously and asks if you want to create a new profile for this user.

6. Choose Yes. cc:Mail displays the first box of the profile setup wizard.

SPECIFYING MAILBOX AND POST OFFICE NAMES

To set the type of connection, the location of your Mobile Mailbox, and the name of your Post Office, follow these steps:

1. In the first dialog box of profile setup wizard, you decide whether you will connect to the cc:Mail post office using a network or a mobile connection. Since we're setting up a mobile connection profile, choose Mobile.

2. Choose Next >. You'll see the second dialog box in the profile setup wizard, in which you must specify the location of the Mobile Mailbox folder (see Figure 18.2). The path cc:Mail suggests for your Mobile Mailbox is a local path, and that's correct since you'll need a local post office while away from the office.

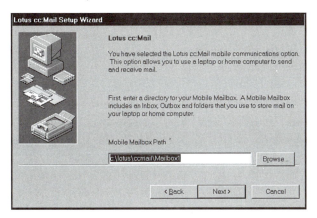

FIGURE 18.2   Specify a path on your traveling computer for your Mobile Mailbox.

3. Choose Next >. On the next screen, type the name of your post office, as provided by your cc:Mail administrator.

SETTING CALLING OPTIONS

To specify the way your modem should work, follow these steps:

1. Choose Next >. On the next screen, the Setup Wizard suggests that the connection type should be Modem, which is correct.

2. Choose Next >. In the next dialog box, type the seven-digit phone number your notebook computer should dial to reach the Post Office.

3. Choose Next >. cc:Mail displays a dialog box asking if you want cc:Mail to determine your modem type and settings.

4. Although it may take a while to complete this procedure, choose Yes. cc:Mail will try to figure out the type of modem you're using, and even if cc:Mail has some trouble, the chances are excellent that cc:Mail will configure your modem correctly. If cc:Mail fails to detect your modem, you'll need to manually select your modem from a list and assign the COM port to which your modem is connected.

5. cc:Mail displays the modem settings it has selected (see Figure 18.3). If you need to make corrections, use the list boxes provided.

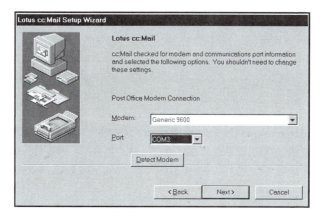

FIGURE 18.3   After detecting your modem, cc:Mail displays the results.

6. Choose Next >. On the next screen, you can choose to make this profile work both in the office and away from the office.

7. Since we set up an "in-office" profile in Lesson 1, choose Next >.

FINALIZING PROFILE SETTINGS

To complete your mobile profile, follow these steps:

1. cc:Mail displays the information it will use to create your profile (see Figure 18.4). If you used a name for yourself

other than one provided to you by your cc:Mail administrator, place a check in the Name check box and click
Change. In the resulting dialog box, type your name as it
was provided to you by your cc:Mail administrator—probably in the format of last name, first name.

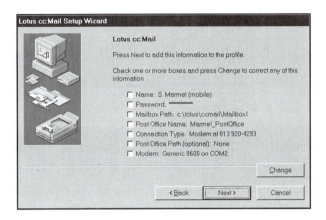

FIGURE 18.4   This profile needs the name changed to match the
one provided by the cc:Mail administrator.

2. Choose Next >. cc:Mail starts the program using your
   new, mobile profile (notice the title bar tells you you're
   using your Mobile Mailbox). You'll see a dialog box asking if you want to connect and get your mail now. To
   continue with our lesson, choose No.

BUILDING A MOBILE PUBLIC ADDRESS BOOK

Now that you have created a mobile profile, you'll quickly notice
that you have Public and Personal Address Books, but they don't
contain the information found in your LAN address books. You
can update the Mobile Address Books using the LAN Address
Books, and you'll want to make this update before you actually
begin traveling.

To update your Mobile Address Books, you'll need to connect to the post office. Follow these steps:

1. Open the Actions menu and choose Connect. cc:Mail displays the dialog box you see in Figure 18.5.

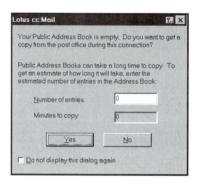

FIGURE 18.5   Use this dialog box to copy address book entries from the Post Office to your Mobile Address Books.

2. Choose Yes. cc:Mail displays the Connection Confirmation dialog box (see Figure 18.6).

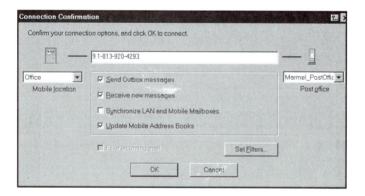

FIGURE 18.6   This dialog box contains the information cc:Mail will use to connect to your Post Office.

3. If necessary, make changes to the phone number displayed at the top of the dialog box and then choose OK.

4. The cc:Mail Background window appears in the upper right corner of your screen (see Figure 18.7).

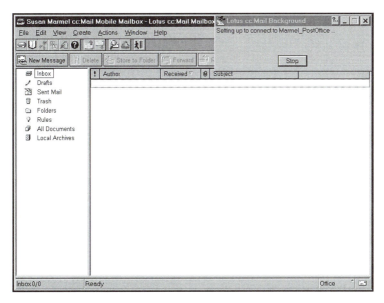

FIGURE 18.7   The cc:Mail Background dialog box shows you what's happening while you are connected to the Post Office.

cc:Mail proceeds to update your Mobile Address Books with the information from the LAN Address Books. Because of the choices selected in the Connection Confirmation dialog box, cc:Mail also downloads to your Mobile Mailbox any messages currently waiting in your LAN Mailbox.

Ending the Connection   To end the connection, click the Stop button in the cc:Mail Background window.

USING THE OUTBOX

As a mobile user, connecting with the Post Office may involve a long distance phone call. To minimize costs, work off-line in cc:Mail until you are ready to send and receive messages. When you work off-line, you don't receive new messages immediately. You'll get them whenever you log on later.

 Off-line   Working in cc:Mail without being connected to the Post Office.

To work off-line, you use the Outbox window to create and store messages you want to send. To open the Outbox, open the Window menu and choose Outbox. cc:Mail displays the Outbox window (see Figure 18.8).

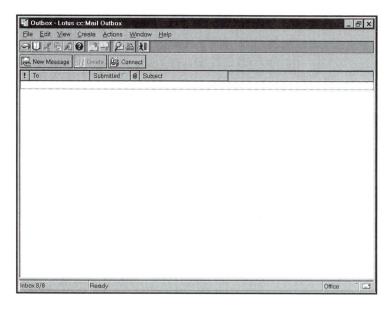

FIGURE 18.8   Use this window to create and store messages you want to send later, when you're connected to the Post Office.

From the Outbox window, click the New Message button to create a new message. Create the new message the same way you learned earlier, in Lesson 7, by supplying an address, subject line, and message text.

CONNECTING FROM DIFFERENT LOCATIONS

Earlier in this lesson, you learned how to connect to the Post Office when you learned how to copy your LAN Address Book entries to your Mobile Address Books. Although we didn't mention it at the time, you used your Office location to make the connection.

 Location A configuration file cc:Mail uses to store information about how your modem should connect your note book computer to the Post Office. In particular, locations contain information about how phone numbers should be dialed.

SWITCHING BETWEEN LOCATIONS

By default, cc:Mail creates three locations for you when you create a mobile profile:

- Office
- Home
- Hotel

The major difference between these locations is the way cc:Mail stores the phone number. See Table 18.1 for the differences in the phone numbers.

TABLE 18.1 PHONE NUMBER SET UP IN DEFAULT LOCATIONS

Office	9 1 555-555-5555
Home	1 555-555-5555
Hotel	8 1 555-555-5555

To switch locations, click the location indicator in the status bar. A pop-up list box appears (see Figure 18.9). Choose the location you want to use.

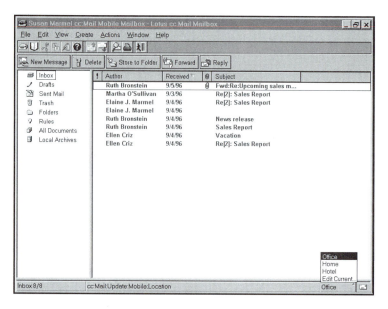

FIGURE 18.9   Use the pop-up list box in the lower-right corner of the mailbox screen to change to a different location.

SETTING UP A LOCATION

Suppose none of the default locations suits your needs. You may want to edit an existing location or even create a new location. For example, many people live in the same area code as their office and therefore don't need to dial 1 and the area code to connect to the Post Office from home. You use the Location dialog box, which contains five different tabs, to make choices about a location. Table 18.2 describes the choices available on each tab.

To edit a location, follow these steps:

1. Open the Actions menu and choose Locations. cc:Mail displays the cc:Mail Location dialog box.

2. Highlight a location to edit and choose Edit. cc:Mail displays the Location dialog box (see Figure 18.10).

New location   To create a new location, choose New. You'll see the same dialog box that you see when editing a location.

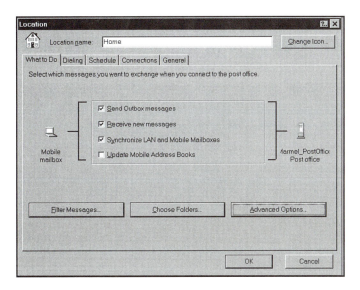

FIGURE 18.10   Use the tabs in this dialog box to make changes to a location.

3. Use Table 18.2 to make choices in this dialog box.

4. Choose OK. cc:Mail redisplays the cc:Mail Location dialog box.

5. Choose OK.

TABLE 18.2   CHOICES AVAILABLE IN THE LOCATION DIALOG BOX.

What to Do	Choose the actions cc:Mail should take when connected to the Post Office: sent Outbox messages, receive new messages, synchronize LAN and Mobil Mailboxes (see the next section for more information), and update Mobile Address Books.
Dialing	Specify the Post Office to which cc:Mail should connect and the phone number to dial. Remember, if you have call waiting service, a *70 prefix should be added to the number so that calls are not interrupted or garbled by this phone company feature.
Schedule	Determine when, if ever, cc:Mail automatically makes connections: On startup, on exit, on sending messages or according to a schedule.
Connections	Modify your communication method or create a new communication method. For example, change the type of modem you're using or the way it behaves.
General	Set general options such as whether cc:Mail displays the Connection Confirmation dialog box when you connect, or whether cc:Mail will notify you when a session is complete.

SYNCHRONIZING MOBILE AND LAN POST OFFICES

As a mobile user, you don't maintain a constant connection with the post office, so you don't always have the most up-to-date information. While you weren't connected, you might have received messages or the Public Address Book might have been updated.

Earlier in this chapter, you learned how to update your Mobile
Address Book. You also can synchronize your Mobile Mailbox
with your LAN mailbox so that the entries in both are the same.
You synchronize the mailboxes by setting options for synchroni-
zation and then connecting to the Post Office. Follow these steps:

1. Open the Actions menu and choose Locations. cc:Mail
   displays the cc:Mail Location dialog box.

2. Highlight the location from which you plan to connect
   and choose Edit. cc:Mail displays the Location dialog box.

3. On the What to Do tab, place a check in the Synchronize
   LAN and Mobile Mailboxes check box. Two buttons,
   Choose Folder and **Advanced Options**, become avail-
   able.

4. Click Choose Folders. cc:Mail displays a dialog box showing that all the folders you have available to synchronize
   are selected. If you want to synchronize only some folders, choose the Selected Folders option button and then
   highlight and add folders from the Available Folders list.
   Choose OK when you finish to return to the Location
   dialog box.

5. Click Advanced Options. cc:Mail displays the Advanced
   Options dialog box (see Figure 18.11).

6. From this dialog box, choose which mailbox (Mobile or
   LAN) will replace the other and also specify how to
   handle deleted messages, folders and Personal Address
   Book entries. Choose OK when you finish to redisplay the
   Location dialog box.

7. Choose OK twice to close both Location dialog boxes and
   return to the Mobile Mailbox window.

To finish the process, connect to the Post Office by choosing Actions, Connect.

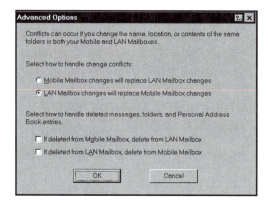

Advanced Options

Conflicts can occur if you change the name, location, or contents of the same folders in both your Mobile and LAN Mailboxes.

Select how to handle change conflicts:

○ Mobile Mailbox changes will replace LAN Mailbox changes

⦿ LAN Mailbox changes will replace Mobile Mailbox changes

Select how to handle deleted messages, folders, and Personal Address Book entries.

☐ If deleted from Mobile Mailbox, delete from LAN Mailbox

☐ If deleted from LAN Mailbox, delete from Mobile Mailbox

OK   Cancel

FIGURE **18.11**   Use this dialog box to determine how cc:Mail should handle differences between your LAN and Mobile Mailboxes.

In this lesson, you learned how to create a mobile profile, to connect to the Post Office, to update your Mobile Address Books, to use the Outbox, to connect from and modify locations, and to synchronize LAN and Mobile Mailboxes. In the next lesson, you'll learn to customize user preferences.

CUSTOMIZING USER SETUP

19

In this lesson, you'll learn to modify preferences for the desktop, the mailbox, confirmation, notification, fonts, spelling, and rules.

MODIFYING THE DESKTOP

If you'd like to change the way the cc:Mail screen looks when you start the program, you can select your preferences in the Desktop section of the cc:Mail Preferences dialog box. Figure 19.1 shows the cc:Mail Preferences dialog box with the Desktop preferences available.

cc:Mail Preferences cc:Mail Preferences is a dialog box you use to modify the way various features operate in cc:Mail. The features are divided within the dialog box for easier management and organization. When you choose a feature on the left side of the dialog box, the right side displays the options you can set for that feature.

TABLE 19.1 DESKTOP PREFERENCES

OPTION	DESCRIPTION
Mailbox	When selected, displays the Mailbox window when you start cc:Mail.
Task Bar	When selected, displays the cc:Mail Task Bar at the top of your screen when you start cc:Mail. You can use the Task Bar to navigate to the Mailbox, the Outbox, or the Workspace.

OPTION	DESCRIPTION
Workspace & Task Bar	When selected, displays the Workspace window (familiar to Lotus Notes users) and the Task Bar when you start cc:Mail.
Mailbox & Task Bar	When selected, displays the Mailbox window and the Task Bar when you start cc:Mail.

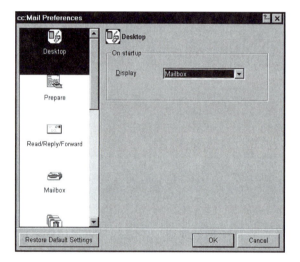

FIGURE 19.1   Use Desktop preferences to determine what you see on your desktop when you start cc:Mail.

To change Desktop preferences, follow these steps:

1. Open the File menu and choose Tools. From the cascading menu that appears, choose User Preferences. The cc:Mail Preferences dialog box appears.

2. In the Preference scroll list on the left side of the dialog box, choose Desktop, if it is not already selected.

3. Referring to Table 19.1, choose any options you want to change.

4. Choose OK to close the dialog box.

SETTING PREFERENCES FOR THE MAILBOX

You can control certain aspects about how your Mailbox window behaves. Using the Mailbox option in the cc:Mail Preferences dialog box (see Figure 19.2), you can control the color of unread messages, the delay time before cc:Mail previews a message in the Preview pane, and whether cc:Mail marks messages you open as "read".

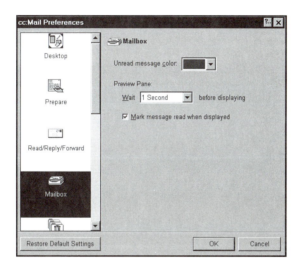

FIGURE 19.2   Set the behavior of your Mailbox window here.

To set Preferences for the Mailbox:

1. Open the File menu and choose Tools. From the cascading menu that appears, choose User Preferences. The cc:Mail Preferences dialog box appears.

2. In the Preference scroll list on the left side of the cc:Mail Preferences dialog box, choose Mailbox.

3. Use the Unread message color list box to choose a different color for messages you haven't read yet.

4. Use the Preview Pane list box to set the time delay cc:Mail waits before displaying a message.

5. Remove the check from the Mark message read when displayed check box if you don't want cc:Mail to change the color of a message you've displayed from the default color blue to black. Note that if you change this option, you may have difficulty distinguishing between messages you have read and messages you haven't read.

6. Choose OK to close the dialog box.

Customizing Confirmation

The Confirmation preferences confirm such actions as deletion, moving, copying, and so on. By default, cc:Mail displays a confirmation dialog box before performing procedures that can be catastrophic or time-consuming to correct.

Deletion Mistakes   It's easy to accidentally delete a folder, archive, mailing list, or other element. Unless you're very sure of yourself, you might want to leave the confirmations for deletions intact to save yourself time, work, and trouble the next time you accidentally hit the Delete key.

Figure 19.3 shows the Confirmation preferences. An X in a check box indicates that the confirmation dialog box will appear when you choose to perform that operation.

To change Confirmation preferences, follow these steps:

1. Open the File menu and choose Tools. From the cascading menu that appears, choose User Preferences. The cc:Mail Preferences dialog box appears.

2. In the Preference scroll list on the left side of the dialog box, choose Confirmation.

3. Make your selections.

4. Choose OK to close the dialog box.

FIGURE 19.3   **FIGURE 19.3**   Choose the confirmations you want for various procedures.

CHANGING NOTIFY PREFERENCES

The Notify preferences govern if and when cc:Mail will notify you when you receive new mail. You can choose how often cc:Mail checks for new mail, where it checks for new mail, and other options.

Figure 19.4 shows the Notify Preferences and Table 19.1 describes the Notify options.

TABLE 19.2   NOTIFY PREFERENCES

OPTION	DESCRIPTION
Enable New Messages	When checked, cc:Mail notifies you when Notification you have new mail.
Notification Method	Choose one, two, or three of the following methods of notification: Tone (sounds a tone) Dialog box (a dialog box appears) Sound (plays a sound file). Your

OPTION	DESCRIPTION
	computer must support sound (i.e., sound card, drivers,and speakers) to use this option.

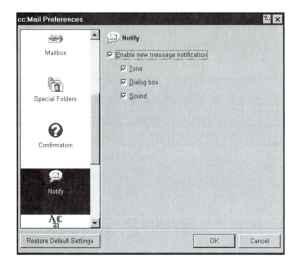

FIGURE 19.4   Choose when and if cc:Mail notifies you of new mail.

To change Notify preferences, follow these steps:

1. Open the File menu and choose Tools. From the cascading menu that appears, choose User Preferences. The cc:Mail Preferences dialog box appears.

2. In the Preferences scroll list, choose Notify.

3. Using Table 19.1, make your selections.

4. Choose OK to accept the changes.

TIP   **Frequency of Notification**   To change how often cc:Mail notifies you of new messages, choose File, Tools, Services. Select the Lotus cc:Mail service and click Properties. In the Check for New Mail Every box, type a number. Choose OK and then Close.

Slow Network? To keep network traffic down, don't set the option to check for messages more frequently than every 6 minutes. The more often it checks, the busier and slower the network becomes.

CHANGING DEFAULT FONTS

You can control the fonts cc:Mail uses in the Address Book, the Mailbox, the Preview Pane, and in message text. Figure 19.5 shows the Fonts Preferences dialog box.

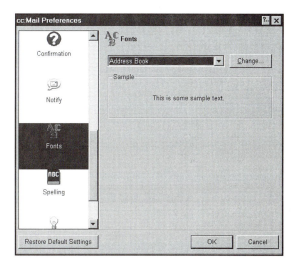

FIGURE 19.5 Use this dialog box to change the fonts cc:Mail uses.

To change Font preferences, follow these steps:

1. Open the File menu and choose Tools. From the cascading menu that appears, choose User Preferences. The cc:Mail Preferences dialog box appears.

2. In the Preferences scroll list, choose Fonts.

3. Open the list box at the top and choose the window for which you want to change fonts.

4. Click the Change button. The Font dialog box appears (see Figure 19.6).

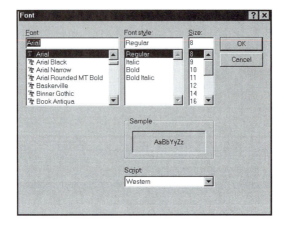

FIGURE 19.6   Make font selections in the Font dialog box.

5. Choose a Font, Font Style, and Size. Then choose OK to redisplay the cc:Mail Preferences dialog box.

6. Choose OK to accept the changes.

CHOOSING A LANGUAGE FOR SPELL CHECKING

You can choose the language cc:Mail uses for spell checking, and you can specify the location of the user dictionary.

User Dictionary   cc:Mail uses a standard dictionary to check spelling. If you decide to add words that you use frequently but aren't found in the standard dictionary, cc:Mail adds new words to your personal dictionary—the User Dictionary.

Figure 19.7 shows the Spelling preferences.

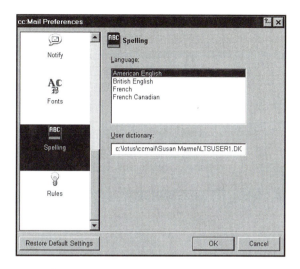

FIGURE 19.7   Set the language cc:Mail uses when checking spelling.

To choose the language cc:Mail uses when checking spelling:

1. Open the File menu and choose Tools. From the cascading menu that appears, choose User Preferences. The cc:Mail Preferences dialog box appears.

2. In the Preferences scroll list, choose Spelling.

3. Make a language selection.

4. If you want to store the User dictionary in a new location, type the path name in the User Dictionary text box.

5. Choose OK to accept the changes.

SETTING PREFERENCES FOR RULES

You can control the behavior of rules. Figure 19.8 shows the Rules Preferences. A check in a check box means the function will operate.

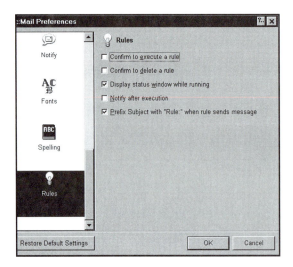

FIGURE 19.8   Determine how rules behave using these options.

To select Rules preferences:

1. Open the File menu and choose Tools. From the cascading menu that appears, choose User Preferences. The cc:Mail Preferences dialog box appears.

2. In the Preferences scroll list, choose Rules.

3. Make your selections.

4. Choose OK to accept the changes.

In this lesson, you learned to modify preferences for the desktop, the mailbox, confirmation, notification, fonts, spelling, and rules. In the next lesson, you'll learn to use Lotus Organizer and the Lotus SmartCenter.

GETTING STARTED WITH ORGANIZER

In this lesson, you'll become acquainted with Organizer and you'll learn to use the Organizer workspace.

GETTING ACQUAINTED WITH ORGANIZER

Organizer is a personal scheduling program that can help you manage your busy life. It's easy to use and has many options and features that make organizing a joy.

cc:Mail installs Organizer automatically for you. To start Organizer, choose the Start button, Programs, Lotus Applications, and Lotus Organizer 2.1.

Figure 20.1 shows the opened Organizer screen.

Organizer is divided into several different parts, each a means to organizing your life:

- **Calendar**   Display the calendar year two days at a time, a week at a time, two weeks at a time, a month at a time, or a year at a time. You can view last year's calendar, next year's calendar, the calendar 10 years ago, or the calendar 10 years from now. In the Calendar, you can divide a day into appointment times, and enter appointments, sound an alarm to remind you of a meeting time, "pencil in" meetings, and warn of conflicts.

- **To Do**   Enter tasks and keep track of overdue, current, future, and completed activities.

- **Addresses and Phone Numbers**   Enter business and/or personal contact information for quick and easy access to anyone anywhere.

- **Planner**   Plan vacations, mark holidays and meetings, track projects, and so on over the course of a month, a year, or several years.

- **Notepad**   Make notes of important deadlines, activities, and other information to save or to throw out when you're done.

- **Anniversary**   Mark important dates for the full year, set an alarm to remind you of a special day, categorize special dates, and more.

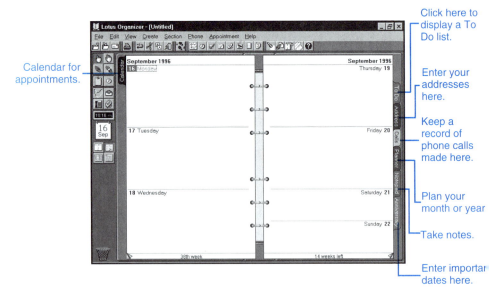

Click here to display a To Do list.

Calendar for appointments.

Enter your addresses here.

Keep a record of phone calls made here.

Plan your month or year

Take notes.

Enter importar dates here.

FIGURE 20.1   Click on any tab to move to that page in the Organizer.

You can save, print, archive, import, and export information from Organizer. You can also send e-mail without closing Organizer—just choose File, Send Mail to open the cc:Mail application window.

UNDERSTANDING THE ORGANIZER WORKSPACE

Most of the elements in the Organizer workspace should be familiar to you: title bar, menu bar, SmartIcons, and so on; however, Organizer adds a few elements to the workspace that may be unfamiliar. Figure 20.2 shows the workspace and various elements of Organizer.

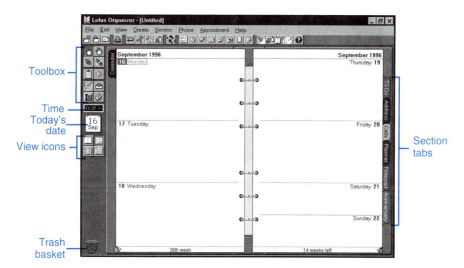

FIGURE 20.2   The workspace in Organizer provides several new tools.

Workspace   The area available for you to use while working in a program. In Organizer, the workspace includes the entire screen area and such elements as the menu, toolbox, view icons, section tabs, and so on.

Table 20.1, describes each of the elements displayed in Figure 20.2.

TABLE 20.1   ORGANIZER SCREEN ELEMENTS

ELEMENT	DESCRIPTION
Toolbox	Provides shortcuts for many Organizer commands and functions.
Time	Displays the current time.
Today's date	Displays the calendar with today's date selected.
View icons	Changes each Organizer section to a different view of that section. For example, the Calendar view icons switch the Calendar from one day per page to one week per page, and so on. The To Do list view icons switch the organization of the To Do section so that tasks are organized, for example, alphabetically or by date.
Section tabs	When clicked, moves Organizer to that section.
Trash basket	Deletes any appointment, text, number, and so on that you drag to it.
SmartIcons	Provides shortcuts to common commands; use bubble help, cartoon-like balloons that contain help information, to identify the function of each.

USING THE TOOLBOX AND VIEW BUTTONS

The toolbox and view buttons provide shortcuts for copying, dialing, moving, printing, and performing other tasks in Organizer. You'll notice that the toolbox contains most of the same tools when you choose different sections in the Organizer book, but the View icons change for each section to provide you with different views appropriate to that section.

Figure 20.3 shows the toolbox and its tools and Table 20.2 describes the toolbox tool buttons. Note that the Insert a New Entry tool changes when you click a different section tab to reflect the type of entry you are making; in the Calendar section, the Insert New Entry tool creates a new appointment, but in the To Do section, the Insert New Entry tool creates a new To Do List item.

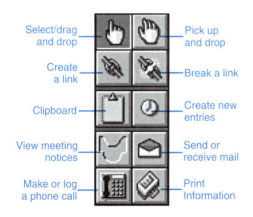

Select/drag and drop
Pick up and drop
Create a link
Break a link
Clipboard
Create new entries
View meeting notices
Send or receive mail
Make or log a phone call
Print Information

FIGURE 20.3   Use the toolbox as a shortcut to many functions.

TABLE 20.2   TOOLBOX TOOLS

TOOL	DESCRIPTION
Select/drag and drop	Select a section tab, calendar entry, and so on; drag and drop entries from one area to another on the same page.
Pick up and drop	Pick up entries and drop to another page.
Create a link	Create a link between entries in different sections of Organizer. For example, you could create a link between a calendar entry and a telephone number or note in the planner.

TOOL	DESCRIPTION
Break a link	Break the link between a calendar entry and another item in Organizer.
Clipboard	Drag and drop an entry to the Clipboard to copy it; drag the entry from the Clipboard to another page or area to paste it.
Insert a New Entry	This Insert icon changes, depending on the selected section tab, to one of the following: Task, Address Record, Call, Page, Event, Anniversary, or Meeting Notices.
View meeting notices	Display meeting notices.
Send or Receive Mail	Send and receive messages between Organizer and cc:Mail.
Make or log phone call	Dial out to make a call or use the log a to keep track of calls.
Print Information	Print selected or displayed data.

The view buttons change depending on the section tab displayed. The bullets below summarize the purpose of the view buttons in each section; the next two lessons describe the view buttons for specific section tabs in greater detail.

- **Calendar tab**   View buttons display one page per day, two pages per week, one page per week, and two pages for a month.

- **To Do tab**   View buttons display priority tabs (1, 2, 3), labeled tabs (Overdue, Current, Future, and Completed), month and year tabs, and alphabetical tab listings.

- **Address tab**   View buttons display all information about an entry, address information, contact information (which includes all phones numbers and e-mail address), or phone numbers.

- **Calls tab**   View buttons display entries by Name, Company, Date, or Category.

- **Planner**   View buttons display the planner as a quarter (three months) per page or as a year per page.

- **Notepad**   View buttons display the Notepad by page number, by title, by date, or by category.

- **Anniversary**   View buttons display entries by month, year, zodiac, or category.

Lose the View Buttons?   If you click the **Calendar** tab, you see the year at a glance and the view buttons disappear. To display the view buttons again, click the Today's date icon.

In this lesson, you became acquainted with Organizer and learned to use the Organizer workspace. In the next lesson, you'll learn to use Organizer's Calendar to schedule meetings.

21

USING THE ORGANIZER CALENDAR AND SCHEDULING MEETINGS

In this lesson, you'll learn to use Organizer's Calendar by entering appointments, rearranging and deleting appointments, and setting appointment options. You'll also learn to schedule meetings with the Calendar.

USING THE CALENDAR

You can use the Organizer Calendar to enter important appointments for this year and for years to come. You can even keep a record of past appointments, meetings, chores, and so on. You can enter names, times, and other information as well as categorize entries, set alarms to notify you of impending appointments, and so on.

Network or Stand-Alone?   Your copy of Organizer may be located on the network server or on your computer. If on the server, you can enter your own appointments, view others' appointments, schedule meetings, and more; however, if you're using the program installed on your computer, all appointments and meetings apply only to you.

ENTERING APPOINTMENTS

You can type into the Calendar pages, no matter which view you're in, to enter notes and other information into specific time slots. Organizer divides the day into time slots for you.

Turn Pages To turn pages in the calendar, position the
selection hand (the mouse pointer) at the bottom, outside
corner of either page. The mouse pointer changes to the
selection hand—a hand pointing left or right. Click the
mouse to turn the page.

TIP

To enter appointments, follow these steps:

1. To display the time slots within any day, click the space
    below the day on a Calendar page. The time slots appear
    (see Figure 21.1).

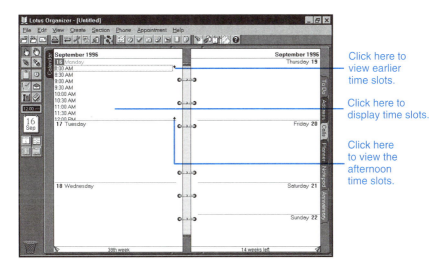

Click here to
view earlier
time slots.

Click here to
display time slots.

Click here
to view the
afternoon
time slots.

FIGURE 21.1   Display time slots so you can enter your appointments.

2. Double-click the time slot at which you want to enter an
    appointment. The Create Appointment dialog box ap-
    pears (see Figure 21.2).

3. Enter the description, name, or other information about
    your appointment in the Description text box.

4. Specify the amount of time you want to reserve for the
    appointment in the Duration text box by clicking the

plus or minus sign next to the box; the default duration is set to one hour.

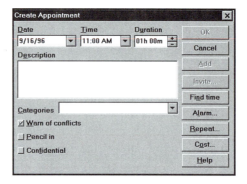

FIGURE 21.2   Enter appointments and/or change the date and time in the Create Appointment dialog box.

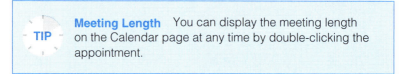

TIP   **Meeting Length**   You can display the meeting length on the Calendar page at any time by double-clicking the appointment.

5. If you want to add another new appointment, on the same day or on another day, choose the Add button. Organizer adds the current appointment to the Calendar and clears the Description box; it's ready for you to enter another.

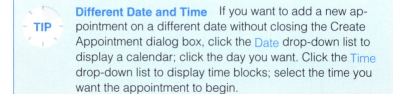

TIP   **Different Date and Time**   If you want to add a new appointment on a different date without closing the Create Appointment dialog box, click the Date drop-down list to display a calendar; click the day you want. Click the Time drop-down list to display time blocks; select the time you want the appointment to begin.

6. When you're done adding appointments, click the OK or Close button.

Conflicting Appointments Don't worry about entering appointment times that conflict with one another. Organizer will warn you so that you can rearrange them.

EDITING APPOINTMENTS AND SETTING OPTIONS

You can change the date, time, duration, description, category, and other information about any appointment by editing that appointment. If you need to move the appointment, simply change the date and/or time; Organizer moves the appointment for you.

For example, you can set an alarm, categorize the appointment, or choose to repeat the appointment. You might want to categorize appointments, for example, to view related appointments by topics.

To edit an appointment, follow these steps:

1. Double-click the entry on the Calendar page.

2. The Edit Appointment dialog box appears (see Figure 21.3).

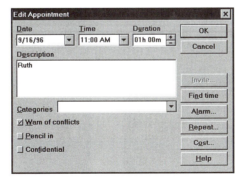

FIGURE 21.3 Move or edit an appointment using the Edit Appointment dialog box.

3. Change any settings, including the following options, and choose OK.

- **Categorize**   Displays the Categorize dialog box from which you choose a category. Choose OK.

- **Alarm**   Displays the Alarm dialog box; choose OK to set the alarm, such as a tone or message.

- **Repeat**   Displays the Repeat dialog box from which you choose how often to repeat the appointment (weekly, monthly, every day, and so on) and the duration or time limit of the repeats. Choose OK to close the dialog box.

- **Cost**   Assigns a cost code to an appointment so that you can track expenses associated with the way you spend your time.

- **Warn Of Conflicts**   When checked, this option tells Organizer to warn you if you try to schedule more than one appointment at the same time.

- **Pencil In**   Displays a pencil beside the appointment so you'll know it's tentative; to turn off the option, select it again.

- **Confidential**   Makes the appointment confidential, so that others who have access to your schedule can't see the appointment.

REARRANGING APPOINTMENTS

You can rearrange appointments using the Edit Appointment dialog box, as described previously, or you can simply drag the appointments to a new location.

When rearranging appointments, you can use any view; the View Month view is the easiest to use. To rearrange appointments, follow these steps:

1. Click the View Month icon.

2. Turn Organizer Calendar pages to move to the month in which you want to rearrange appointments (see Figure 21.4).

Click here to view the month across two pages.

Click here to view the previous month.

Click here to view the next month.

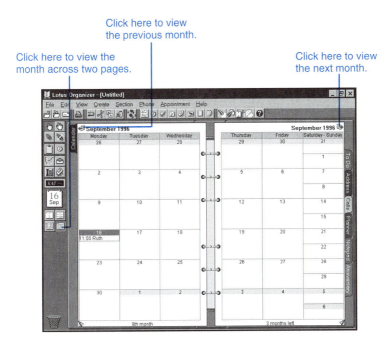

FIGURE 21.4 Viewing the entire month makes scheduling easier.

3. Click the appointment you want to move, and drag it to the block representing the new appointment date. As you drag the text, the selection hand changes to a clock. Release the mouse button to drop the appointment into its new location.

TIP **Move Appointments Between Months?** To move an appointment to another month, select the appointment and use Cut and Paste editing methods.

4. To change the time of the appointment, click the selected appointment once. The time bar appears (see Figure 21.5).

5. To change the time, position the mouse pointer on the beginning time until you see the double-headed arrow. Drag the time up or down until it displays the appropriate time. Drag the ending time to the appropriate place on the time bar to adjust the duration of the meeting.

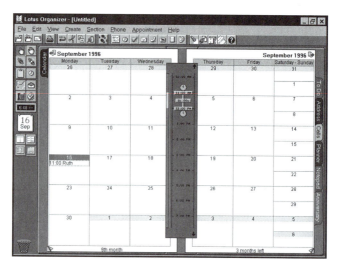

FIGURE 21.5 You can lengthen or shorten the duration of the meeting or change the time altogether.

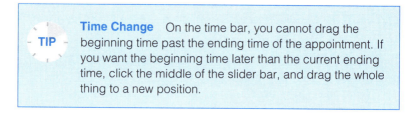

TIP

Time Change On the time bar, you cannot drag the beginning time past the ending time of the appointment. If you want the beginning time later than the current ending time, click the middle of the slider bar, and drag the whole thing to a new position.

6. Click anywhere on the Calendar page to hide the time bar.

DELETING APPOINTMENTS

To delete an appointment, select it and press the Delete key; Organizer deletes the appointment immediately with no warning. Alternatively, you can drag the appointment to the Trash Basket. You do not have to "empty" the Trash Basket; Organizer immediately deletes anything placed in the can.

You can undo an appointment deletion by pressing Ctrl+Z, as long as you haven't performed another action or task since deleting the appointment.

USING THE CALENDAR TO SCHEDULE MEETINGS

Using the Organizer Calendar, you can invite your co-workers to meetings as well as receive invitations from others to their meetings.

SETTING UP A MEETING

Typically, when you schedule meetings in Organizer, you decide when, where, and who will be invited. You set the date, time, duration, and description of meetings in the Create Appointment dialog box. If you're using a network version of Organizer that supports group scheduling, you also can "invite" people to attend.

After you set up a meeting, you can invite others to join you by following these steps:

1. In the Create Appointment dialog box, choose the Invite button. The Schedule Meeting dialog box appears.

2. You can edit the date, time, or duration, if you want.

3. From the list of attendees, choose those you want to attend your meeting. As you add names to the list, Organizer displays the attendee names along with their available time.

4. Enter the people or resources you want to participate in the meeting.

5. Choose the meeting room from the Room drop-down box and then choose OK.

6. In the dialog box that appears, enter a description of the meeting and choose OK.

Organizer sends a meeting invitation to those attendees on your list.

No list of Attendees?   If you are using a network version of Organizer supporting group scheduling, the Invite button will be available and the list of possible attendees will display when you click it. If your version of Organizer does not support group scheduling, you'll want to skip past the remainder of this lesson. If you're not sure, see your system administrator.

CANCELING, CHANGING, OR CONFIRMING THE MEETING

You can cancel a meeting that you scheduled or change information about it. When you cancel or change a meeting, Organizer automatically sends a notice to all attendees. You can also confirm a meeting a couple of days before hand, just to remind attendees of the upcoming meeting.

To cancel a meeting, go to the Calendar page on which the meeting is displayed and drag the meeting to the trash can. Organizer sends notices to the attendees that the meeting has been canceled.

To change or confirm a meeting you scheduled, follow these steps:

1. Go to the Calendar in Organizer and select the meeting.
2. Choose Appointment, Status.
3. Edit any of the details you want to change, or
4. choose the Confirm button to confirm.
5. Choose OK.

Organizer sends the attendees a notice either informing them of the changes or confirming the meeting.

ACCEPTING OR DECLINING AN INVITATION

When you receive an invitation to a meeting, the hands in the meeting notices icon shake to notify you. You can either accept or decline the meeting invitation.

To accept or decline the meeting invitation, follow these steps:

1. When you notice the shaking hands icon, choose File, Meeting Notices.

2. In Notices, double-click the meeting invitation.

3. To accept the invitation, choose the Reply tab and enter a message. Choose Accept and then choose OK. Organizer adds the meeting to your Calendar and sends your response to the chairperson.

4. To decline the invitation, choose the Reply tab and enter a message. Choose Decline and then choose OK. Organizer sends your response to the chairperson.

VIEWING THE STATUS OF ATTENDEES

After you accept an invitation to the meeting, you can check to see who else will attend the meeting.

To view the attendee status, follow these steps:

1. In the Calendar, select the meeting and choose Appointment, Status. A dialog box appears displaying the status of the attendees.

2. Choose Close when you're done.

In this lesson, you learned to use the Calendar and to schedule meetings in Organizer. In the next lesson, you'll learn to enter addresses, to use the Planner, and to use the To Do List.

LESSON 22

USING THE ADDRESS BOOK, THE PLANNER, AND THE TO DO LIST

In this lesson, you'll learn to create addresses, edit addresses, use the Planner, and use the To Do list.

USING THE ADDRESS BOOK

The Address section of Organizer presents an address book in which you can store business and personal addresses. You can also add other information such as job titles, fax numbers, e-mail addresses, notes, spouse's names, children's names, and more.

CREATING ADDRESSES

You can add one or more addresses to the Address section at a time. Entering an address is as easy as filling in a form. All addresses you enter have two tabs: one for business and one for home; you can fill in information for either or both tabs.

To create addresses, follow these steps:

1. Select the Address section tab of the Organizer.

2. Double-click the first page of the Address section. The Create Address dialog box appears (see Figure 22.1).

3. Select the tab you want to complete, either Business or Home, and enter the information as specified. You do not have to fill in all information.

4. When you finish, choose OK to add the address and close the dialog box; alternatively, choose the Add button to add the address and keep the dialog box open so that you can create another address.

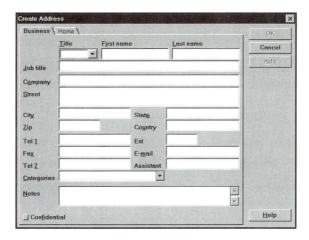

FIGURE 22.1   You can create an address in either the Business or Home tab of the dialog box.

Figure 22.2 shows one entry in the Address book.

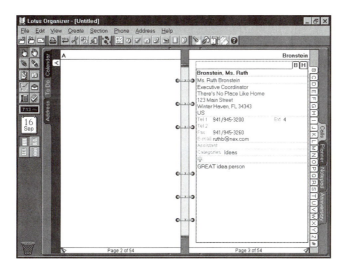

FIGURE 22.2   You can view names, addresses, phone numbers, and so on for home and business.

EDITING ADDRESSES

You can easily edit an entry's name, address, phone number, and other information at any time.

To edit an address entry, double-click the entry on the Address page and the Edit Address dialog box appears. Make any changes, deletions, or other modifications and choose OK.

To delete an address, drag the entry to the Trash Basket.

Accidentally deleted an entry?   Organizer immediately deletes any entries in the Trash Basket, but you can press Ctrl+Z to undo your last action and reinstate the entry.

USING PLANNER

Planner presents the yearly calendar for extensive advance project or activity preparation. Using Planner, you can block off your vacation, mark trade show or conference days, plan company projects, and more. As you plan, you can see how busy each week, month, and year will be.

To use Planner, follow these steps:

1. Click the Planner tab of Organizer. The Planner for the current year appears (see Figure 22.3).

2. To block time for a project, vacation, or other activity, click the event button and move the mouse pointer, which will be shaped like a highlighter, to the first date of the event.

Which Date?   Keep your eye on the date box just above the event buttons as you move the mouse across the blocks so you'll know the exact date.

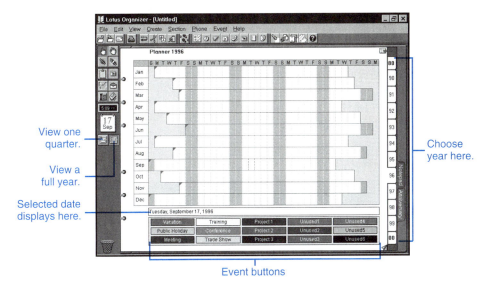

View one quarter.

View a full year.

Selected date displays here.

Choose year here.

Event buttons

FIGURE 22.3 Use the Planner to organize your week, month, or year.

3. Drag the highlighter to the end of the block of time. Planner marks the area with a color band corresponding to the event button. If necessary, you can drag the end of the highlighter block back or forward, or you can drag the block to another location on the Planner. You also can drag the block to the Trash Basket to delete it.

TIP   **Another Method**   If you prefer, you can double-click any day in the Planner to display the Create Event dialog box. Choose the event type, dates, and add comments, if you like.

Using the To Do List

The To Do list provides you with various ways of cataloging your chores, duties, and tasks. You can list chores by priority, by labels, by dates, or by category.

CREATING A TASK

You cannot flip through the tabs of the To Do section until you create at least one task.

To create a task, follow these steps:

1. Choose the To Do section tab. The To Do section appears (see Figure 22.4).

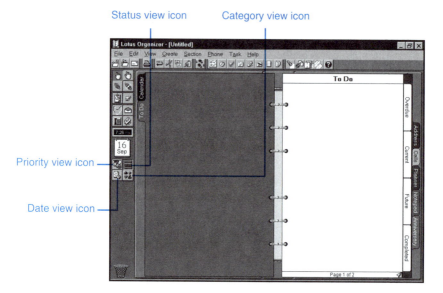

FIGURE 22.4   Record and organize your To Do list.

2. Double-click anywhere on the To Do section divider or page. The Create Task dialog box appears (see Figure 22.5).

3. In Description, identify the task. You can use a name, words, phrases, sentences, any descriptions that help you recognize the task.

4. In Date, optionally enter a start and due date in the Start and Due text boxes.

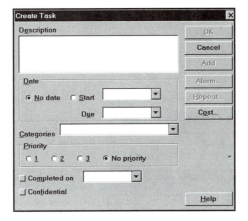

FIGURE 22.5   Create a task to add to the To Do list.

TIP   **Shortcut**   When you click in the Start or Due text box, today's date appears. You can enter the correct date or use the drop-down list box to display the calendar and choose a date.

5. In Priority, optionally choose 1 for high priority, 2 for medium, or 3 for low priority; alternatively, choose No Priority.

6. Choose OK to add the task, or choose the Add button to add the task to the To Do list and leave the Create Task dialog box open to add another task.

Organizer adds the tasks to the list. Figure 22.6 shows a sample task list. To view Overdue or Future tasks, click that tab and the page turns; similarly, use the tabs to view additional pages in which ever view you're using.

TIP   **Turn the Pages**   Organizer only adds as many pages as you need to contain your tasks.

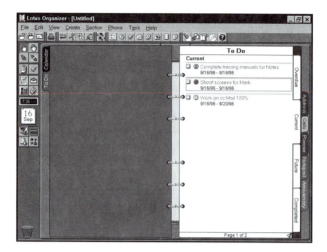

FIGURE 22.6   Current projects are listed in the To Do list.

MANAGING TASKS

Tasks are easy to manage in Organizer; you can edit, delete, and complete a task quickly.

To edit a task, double-click it, and the Edit Task dialog box appears. Change the description, dates, categories, priority, or add an alarm, and so on.

To mark a task as completed, click the gray check box beside the task; a check mark appears to indicate you have finished that task. If the divider tabs in the To Do list section contain labels (Current, Overdue, Future, and Completed), completed tasks move to the Completed tab.

To delete a task, drag it to the Trash Basket.

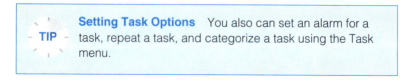

Setting Task Options   You also can set an alarm for a task, repeat a task, and categorize a task using the Task menu.

In this lesson, you learned to use the Address book, the Planner, and the To Do List.

INDEX